Charles Decker

Coauthor of the international bestseller *Beans*

LESSONS FROM THE
Hive

The Buzz

on Surviving and

Thriving in an

Ever-Changing Workplace

This publication is designed to provide accurate and authoritative information in regard to the subject matter covered. It is sold with the understanding that the publisher is not engaged in rendering legal, accounting, or other professional service. If legal advice or other expert assistance is required, the services of a competent professional should be sought.

Vice President and Publisher: Cynthia A. Zigmund
Acquisitions Editor: Jonathan Malysiak
Senior Project Editor: Trey Thoelcke
Interior Design: Lucy Jenkins
Cover Design: Design Solutions
Typesetting: the dotted i

Published by Dearborn Trade Publishing
A Kaplan Professional Company

Printed in the United States of America

04   05   06   10   9   8   7   6   5   4   3   2   1

Library of Congress Cataloging-in-Publication Data

Decker, Charles, 1952-
    Lessons from the hive : the buzz on surviving and thriving in an ever-changing workplace / Charles Decker.
        p.   cm.
    ISBN 0-7931-9186-6
    1. Organizational change.   2. Consolidation and merger of corporations.   3. Management.   I. Title.
HD58.8.D427 2004
650.1′3—dc22   2004006706

Dearborn Trade books are available at special quantity discounts to use for sales promotions, employee premiums, or educational purposes. Please call our Special Sales Department to order or for more information at 800-621-9621 ext. 4444, e-mail trade @dearborn.com, or write to Dearborn Trade Publishing, 30 South Wacker Drive, Suite 2500, Chicago, IL 60606-7481.

To EBG and JAG
For more than they know

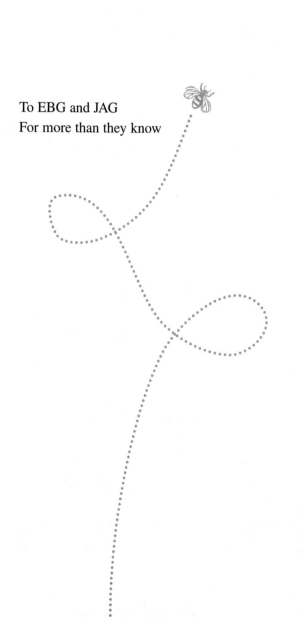

CONTENTS

FOREWORD

FABLES, PARABLES, AND ALLEGORIES have been part of our society since the advent of language itself. They play an enormous role in the Bible, for example, and in the storytelling tradition that is passed from generation to generation.

Using the fable format to underscore basic business principles is a relatively modern invention and many of my colleagues (myself included) use them often in our work. I cannot think of a less-threatening way to impart information and reinforce learning. The problem in the past has been that so few of them reflected the day-to-day realities of running a business.

Not so with *Lessons from the Hive.* Using spare prose and real-world situations, *Beans* coauthor Charles Decker introduces us to characters so well drawn and three-dimensional that we immediately relate to and empathize with their dilemmas. It is also a flat-out fun story that will have you smiling in recognition of the characters' foibles while shaking your head, frustrated with their actions.

Clients tell me almost every day how much they would like a new book about managing change that's not so "dumbed down" they can't give it to their employees. I think we have a new contender with *Lessons from the Hive.*

I also love the fact that the author looks at his characters in a much more holistic way. I found the main character, Dana

Carswell, rather poignant, as she typifies the plight in which many women find themselves every day balancing work and family while also facing the increasing pressure to do even more.

In addition to chronicling an actual business undergoing the throes of change, *Lessons from the Hive* also includes questions for group discussion that highlight the book's main points in a refreshing new way. While you will no doubt have a tendency to race through this immediately engaging story, take time after each chapter to turn to the questions in the back of the book. I guarantee you will have a more enriching experience because of it—and so will your team.

I challenge you to read *Lessons from the Hive* with an open mind about how changing your attitude can make an enormous difference in how your day turns out. I think it has the power to change the perceptions of your work, your boss, your career, your family, and your life itself. Read on and see if you don't agree.

—Beverly Kaye, Ph.D., founder and CEO, Career Systems International, Inc., and coauthor, *Love It, Don't Leave It*

AUTHOR'S NOTE

THIS IS A FICTIONALIZED ACCOUNT of real people running a real business. In the process of storytelling, as well as to protect the privacy of the people involved, names have been changed. Some of the events depicted are also the product of invention. The author thanks those individuals who have shared their stories with him over the years.

FOR THE SAKE OF CHANGE

THE SOUND OF the oldies station came blaring forth the moment Dana Carswell turned the key in the ignition of her family's Subaru wagon. Her teenage son Chris must have been listening to the station at max volume when he drove his buddies home from their band rehearsal last night. *I love those oldies too*, she thought. *Maybe the reason we have so many fights is because we have so much in common.*

She knew she was going to be late to work, again, but at least she had half an hour or so of time to herself—away from the kids, away from the office, away. Maybe the hits of her adolescence could somehow transport her into another, less complicated time.

"Here's one going out to Melissa Turner from her team at Calico Corners," the DJ said, as Dana hurried to adjust the volume. "It's the Mamas and the Papas—gone but not forgotten."

Monday, Monday
So good to me.
Monday morning, it was all
I hoped it would be-e-e . . .

If only, Dana thought. She had already decided that this Monday was going to be a total bitch—just like almost all the others. *If* her *team sent the Velvet Hammer a song, what would it be?* she wondered. *Probably that one by Kenny Rogers about knowing when to hold 'em and when to fold 'em. They don't have a clue how many times I've wanted to fold 'em.*

It had been a rocky three years at Bee Natural, the upscale candle company Dana had worked for since its founding more than twenty years ago. Sales were up substantially over last year, which was amazing in this tough economy, but profits were down. Employee turnover had increased since Jeanne Rasmussen had taken the reins as CEO following Bee Natural's acquisition by a larger consumer-products company, but that was probably to be expected. Jeanne seemed smart and capable, but she needed work in the interpersonal relations area.

When she first came in to head the transition team after the acquisition, *before* they craftily announced her official appointment as CEO, Dana expected Jeanne to suggest some pretty radical changes, but she was frankly unprepared for some of the recommendations Jeanne had made. And on Friday, Dana was told Jeanne expected her marketing director to have a slick PowerPoint presentation ready for the board of directors meeting coming up in just ten days. It was the first time Dana would be involved in a directors' meeting since the acquisition, but Jeanne carefully explained to her that her "archival knowledge" of the company (a nice way to say she was an old-timer, she thought) would be vital in having the new board understand more of where the company had been, and where it was going.

They'll get a presentation, all right, Dana thought. *They just don't know that I'm probably the only one around here willing to tell the truth about things. They're going to get a mountainside of truth, all come tumbling down around them. Jeanne will be sorry she ever asked me to be involved in this meeting.*

Dana's cell phone suddenly chirped and, as much as she hated to multitask while driving, she thought she had better see who could be calling this early in the morning. Didn't people know she was *busy* in the morning getting her husband and the kids ready for their day? The caller ID told her it was Matt Parker, Bee Natural's director of sales, and the one who always found a way, somehow, to set her teeth on edge. She considered passing on the call, but hoped that Matt might have some new office "skinny" for her. He was usually at work long before anybody, mostly to escape the needy kids he and his wife were trying to raise, though he told everybody he needed to be in the office to "get an early start on the day." The good thing about that was that Matt always had an early preview of what lay ahead at the office.

"Matt, you dog. You've beat me to work again." The cheeriness in Dana's voice thinly masked a deep resentment. "I've given up trying to compete with you."

"No need to compete, Dana. I'm just here early to give people who need it a heads up. I didn't want you to come in and have your mood ruined by reading your e-mail."

"That's so thoughtful of you, Matt. So you call me and ruin my drive to work. Thanks. But I guess that's what cell phones are all about, isn't it? Go ahead and spill it—what evil is lurking in my in-box today?"

"Hey, I'm only thinking of you. I know that you've got a lot going on with all your family stuff, and that you could do without surprises at work. Particularly bad ones."

"Matt, get to the point, okay? What's going to ruin my day?"

"Jeanne has posted the board meeting's agenda on the intranet and you're up first. Plus, she wants to have a preliminary meeting with all of us today. You and Todd get a hearing with the High Priestess together, lucky you."

"Is that all? You called me to tell me that? Todd and I have some qualms about the new direction of the company, so I won't mind sharing the floor with him one bit. In fact, I'm glad I'll have a little moral support with Jeanne breathing down my neck. That news is a little bit underwhelming, if you ask me."

"Oh . . . I guess I forgot to tell you the good part," Matt said. "Jeanne has invited a business reporter to spend some time with us this week, interviewing us about how well the company is managing the merger, starting new product lines, and all that other hooey. I guess we'll have to put on a big smile and figure out how to get everything done for the board meeting while taking time to talk pretty for him."

Oh brother, Dana thought. *This is all probably more PR that Jeanne has orchestrated to make nice with the board.*

"But I have to take two afternoons off this week to go to family counseling," she said. "The timing couldn't be worse."

"I remember you mentioning something about that, but I hope it won't interfere with you training our new employee."

Oh my God, Dana thought. *I totally forgot about our new admin. She's starting today and I am going to be late—again.*

"Not at all," Dana said too quickly. "She's not in yet, is she?"

"Not yet, but if she gets in before you do, I'll start going over some things with her myself—give her the lay of the land around here, sort of."

"Matt, if you don't mind, could you have her spend some time with HR first? I think if we're going to share an employee it's important that we start off on equal footing."

"Well, I hate to see her sitting around just because you're late," Matt said, as if he wanted to turn the knife a little further. "I can cover for you a few minutes, but then she's going to think we don't have our act together if we don't give her some 'quality time' PDQ."

"Matt, I'll be there by 9:30. The world is not going to stop if she has to wait a few minutes for us."

"Okay, okay. I'll give her an annual report to read or something. Just try to get a move on. At least I've already given you the bad news of the day."

Yes, you have, Dana thought. The only worse news was that she would probably have to have lunch with him—and their new employee, of course.

Monday, Monday
Can't trust that day.

Three trips around the parking lot had made her even later, so Dana decided to park in one of the visitors' spaces. *They have far more spaces than they need,* Dana thought. *And way too many disabled slots. Nobody will even notice.*

Just as she was unbuckling her seatbelt and checking her lipstick, Todd Ramos, the company's new products guy, knocked on the driver's side window. "Dana, I saw you circling out here from my window. Our meeting with Jeanne is in less than half an hour and I need to go over some stuff with you first."

"Todd, I'm sorry. I'm a little late, okay? I just heard about the meeting with Jeanne, and I have to go spend at least a few minutes with my new assistant. Matt's probably already got her in his clutches."

"Yeah, I saw him walking her around the halls," Todd confirmed. "You should have set your alarm a little earlier. Or maybe you should have checked your e-mail over the weekend."

"Shoulda coulda woulda," Dana responded. "I'll meet you in your office in fifteen minutes."

He's got some nerve telling me how to play the office game. He doesn't have a clue what it's like to get everybody ready in the morning.

As Dana passed the receptionist's desk, she heard the familiar voice of Matt Parker introducing *his* new assistant, Nikki Cavanagh, to the head of security.

"She's going to need a badge and a parking pass right away," Matt said. "I'll send her back at 11:00 or so to get her photo taken. I want to introduce her around first."

"And I want to spend some time with her as well," Dana interjected, peeved that Matt had taken the lead once again on an employee whose salary would be coming out of both their budgets. "I would have been here earlier but traffic was horrendous. Nikki, it's good to see you again."

"Thank you," Nikki said. "I'm sorry you had traffic problems. I guess I'm lucky that I live so close I can bike to work. I won't be needing that parking pass, but I will come back later for one of those glamorous office photos. Dana, do you want some coffee? I'll be glad to get some for you."

"No, thanks anyway. I have a meeting in just a few minutes with our new CEO and I don't think I need to be more wired than I already am. But I have to go over some things first with our head of product development. In fact, why don't you come with me? Might as well have one of those baptisms by fire."

"Dana, I don't think that's a very good idea," Matt said. "She's brand new and you know there are some things that need to get done to make sure she gets on board properly. Go on to your meeting and I'll take her to HR and get the paperwork started."

Nikki caught the ice-cold look that passed between Matt and Dana. "Hey, I'm flexible. Just tell me where you want me."

"Fine, Matt," Dana said. "In fact, that is a good idea. But I think it would be nice if we could all three meet for lunch—my treat."

"Ah, no can do," Matt said. "Todd and I need to get together about the focus groups we have scheduled for later this month. I'll let you two have some 'girl talk' time together."

"I should be involved in those focus groups too," Dana said, "so please make sure you at least copy me on any e-mail exchanges between the two of you, okay?"

"No prob. Will do. We've got plenty of time. My afternoon is going to be pretty much taken up with that business reporter I told you about, so feel free to have a nice long lunch together."

"Then I'll see you right around noon, Nikki," Dana said. "If you have any questions, I'm sure Matt has the answers. If not, spend some time with the employee orientation stuff that's on the intranet. It's very helpful."

My God, Dana thought, *I haven't even made it to my office yet and it already has all the makings of a horrible day. I'll have to talk to Nikki at lunch about Matt's self-serving tactics. I don't want her to get caught up in the nasty politics he creates.*

"Dana, I'm ready when you are," Todd said, returning from the employee cafeteria and grabbing her free arm. "We're going to have to get a move on before we see Jeanne. No time for dawdling around here."

Dawdling—right. Maybe I could find a minute in my schedule to actually make it to the ladies' room. Then again, maybe not.

Todd shuffled the papers on his desk and started putting up some designs for new packaging as Dana sat and grabbed a pad and ballpoint from his desk.

"You know, I feel like we are really rushing this, and it's all because of that board meeting next week," Dana said. "Why did you think we needed to talk before meeting with Jeanne?"

"I guess I feel like I need an ally in all this, Dana. I want this company to make it. You've been here a long time and I feel you have more of a stake in it than just about anybody. I don't trust Matt to support a new initiative, yet I think that's our only hope for survival. I need you to tell Jeanne that moving in a dramatic new direction is the only way we can stay afloat."

"Aren't you being a bit dramatic? We know we have to grow, but candles are our business. That's what we make; that's what we sell. What kind of 'new direction' are you talking about?"

"I'll save that for our meeting with Jeanne, but I just wanted to forewarn you that I am going to make some suggestions about new product lines that are a bit 'out there.' I need your support."

"Todd, I think you're smart and talented, and I know you miss your time in the beauty products world, but I think companies that lose sight of their core business often fail." Dana rose suddenly. "Just because I've been here a while doesn't mean I'm willing to support the company taking some major risks that have no chance of paying off."

"Just hear me out, Dana. And please don't object too much, even if you don't agree at first. It's important that Jeanne feels there will be support from the management team about making some changes around here."

"There have already been plenty of changes, Todd, and I don't know that I'm ready for more. I'll hear you out, but don't plan on me waving your flag if I don't agree with what you're suggesting."

"That's fair. But Matt is too caught up in his own agenda—slouching towards retirement, if you know what I mean—to be much help. You're my best shot. That's why I asked Jeanne to meet with just the two of us."

"Could you ask her for a little more notice next time?"

A meeting with Jeanne Rasmussen always seemed like an audience with the Pope, in Dana's mind at least. In all fairness, though, Jeanne was likable enough, and seemed to give people a chance to make their points before coming to a decision herself. Her no-nonsense approach sat well with Dana, and she particularly liked the way that Jeanne's meetings never lasted more than an hour—at most. She was unprepared for Jeanne's demeanor this Monday morning, however.

"Okay, folks, I've got a busy calendar today. Todd asked for this meeting so I assume he has briefed you on what he has to say, Dana. I can give you fifteen minutes—I'm afraid there's no time for catching up on everybody's weekend."

Oh boy, Dana thought. *She's off to the races. She's probably brought out the stopwatch for this one.*

"Actually, Jeanne, Dana *doesn't* know much about why I called this meeting. In fact, I feel like I'm practicing a little deception. Dana also doesn't know what you and I have been talking about for the last few weeks, but I felt like I wanted to bring her on board. Frankly, Dana, we need your support."

Taken aback somewhat, Dana said, "I feel like I have been set up a little. If this is a meeting about strategic direction, I think the rest of the management team should be here too."

"No, Dana," Jeanne said. "We're not quite ready for that. I've been under the gun from our parent company to usher in a whole new era here. I thought the best way to do that would be with a new product line, and I've been meeting privately with Todd so he could begin his background research. We've been talking about going into the personal care business."

"With beeswax?" Dana asked incredulously. "We make candles. People know us for high-quality, all-natural, long-burning candles. That's what we do. Our products come from the hive. What do we know about personal care?"

"Todd knows quite a bit about that industry, and he has already presented me some interesting ideas for using beeswax as a major component in lip balm, for instance, and moisturizing creme and other skin products. We've got to expand, and the personal care industry is enormous and growing."

"But there are all kinds of regulatory issues that come into play if you're talking about what people put on their skin," Dana said. "I agree that we need to expand, but isn't this pretty radical?"

"Todd's background is chemistry," Jeanne answered. "He knows compounds, and he also knows how to use natural materials in products that people will pay a premium for if they think they are helping the environment. Yes, we are going to have to get involved with the FDA, and yes, there are going to be some areas in which we just can't compete, but our new owners have given their blessing to pursuing this direction. They understand consumer behavior. It could be painful, at least for the short term. It might mean changing the name of the company, and perhaps even moving to a more labor-friendly state. Todd and I thought it would be vital to have your support. You've been here a long time and you have long-term relationships. You also know the customer base cold. Most of those customers are gift shops and specialty stores that sell many other kinds of products, including personal care. I know this means a major overhaul of the company, but we need you to be on board with it. This is going to be the primary topic for the board meeting next week, so we didn't want to blindside you."

"Jeanne, this *is* strategic," Dana said. "This *is* the kind of stuff we should be talking about with the entire management team, particularly Matt."

"Some people won't be able to make the transition," Jeanne said with a look of concern. "We know that you speak your mind and can influence how the troops feel about these changes. We need you to be with us."

"Of course I'm with you." Dana felt the need to be a team player but also concern about what she had just learned. "I think we have to be careful how we manage the information flow to the rest of the company, that's all. Some people are not comfortable with all this change."

"Exactly, Dana." Todd looked straight at her. "You're one of them. But if people see you embracing change, they will be better able to come along for the ride."

"Wow, my mind is reeling," Dana said, starting to rise. "There seems like so much more to talk about. Todd and I should go over this subject off-line, because I have more questions and concerns. And I think we need to be mindful of Matt's feelings. He's going to feel totally left out. Has anybody thought of that? He and I share an employee now, you know."

"Let me take care of Matt," Jeanne said. "Let's keep all this to ourselves, for the moment. Peter Abrams, the reporter who's writing the story on the company, knows a little bit about it but I've told him how sensitive he needs to be until we announce it to the company as a whole. I'm most concerned about Matt, and it may be that he will surprise us and be an advocate. We'll just have to wait and see."

With a dismissive swoop of Jeanne's hand, the "audience" was over.

"Dana," Todd said, stopping outside Jeanne's office and seeming to carefully phrase his words. "I really hope you can join us. Jeanne is taking a big personal risk on this. Give it some thought, and let's you and I meet later today and talk over some of the specifics. I need an ally; Jeanne needs a win. The company needs a win."

"I think I just need some time for this to sink in, Todd. I agree with you in principle, but I'm not exactly thrilled with some of the tactics I'm seeing in play here. I have a lunch planned with my new assistant. How about we meet tomorrow afternoon? Let me give all this some thought."

Blindsided? What an understatement, Dana thought. *And how dare you say that I resist change! I deal with change just fine—but not changing for the sake of change. You're going to have to prove you have the goods, Mr. Chemist Man. Or I'll be melting some candle wax on* your *skin!*

See page 97 for reading group discussion questions for this chapter.

2

WICKS AND STICKS

· ·

AS DANA AND NIKKI made their way past the reception area toward Dana's illegally parked car, they heard the receptionist inform Matt of business reporter Peter Abrams's arrival.

"Well, he's here *now*," the receptionist said into her headset, the anxiety apparent in her voice. "He said he's early but was hoping to meet with you now." Peter listened nearby.

"Let's wait a sec," Dana whispered conspiratorially to Nikki. "This might get good."

"I'll tell him," the receptionist told Matt, "but when do you think you might be free?"

"He pulls this stuff all the time," Dana said to Nikki with a stinging tone of rebuke in her voice. "I've had to cover for him thousands of times when he's double-booked himself. You're going to have a tough time managing his calendar."

"I'm sorry, sir, but Mr. Parker has a lunch planned with our director of new products," the receptionist told the reporter.

"He says he can get with you around 2:00. It's probably best if you come back then."

"I'll do that," Peter responded. "I was just hoping to get some background on my story before meeting with your CEO tomorrow. She told me I could have unlimited access to your management team."

"I'm Dana Carswell, and I apologize for my colleague," Dana said, stepping forward and extending her hand. "This is Nikki Cavanagh, my new assistant. I'm looking forward to filling you in on the company's history. I've been around since the Mayflower, people like to remind me."

"Pleased to meet you both. Maybe I was a bit presumptuous in thinking I could get a head start on my story. Matt told me last week to drop by anytime. I guess he was just being affable."

"Oh, that's Matt. Always being the jolly good fellow. I think he forgets that people take him up on those invitations. I can't tell you how many times I've had to. . . . Oh, never mind. His intentions are good. I'll look forward to opening up the vault for you, so to speak. We're meeting Wednesday afternoon, isn't it?"

"Good memory, Dana. Yes, you're on my schedule for Wednesday. I understand you're the company's human scrapbook."

"That's one of the things they call me." Some bitterness had crept into Dana's voice. "I might know one or two things about the *future* of the company, too, you know."

"I didn't mean . . ." Peter stammered, his face reddening.

"No worries, Peter. I'll be happy to give you some historical background on the company. I know where all the bees are buried."

Todd Ramos sauntered into Matt Parker's office just as Matt was hanging up the phone.

"Hey, Todd, we're still on for lunch, right? I just put off that pushy reporter so you could catch me up on your meeting with Jeanne and Dana."

"Absolutely. We can grab a bite in the cafeteria, can't we? I have to admit I feel like I need an ally right now. Dana just showed her fangs to Jeanne. She just can't get with the program."

"What else is new?" Matt said. "I can tell you that Jeanne is not going to put up with her BS, and I'm sick of covering for her. You know that she and I don't exactly have a mutual admiration society going. She's probably stabbing me in the back with our new employee right now."

Dana unlocked the passenger-side door for Nikki and began tossing the residue from the previous night's band rehearsal into the back seat.

"Don't worry about it, Dana," Nikki said. "I ride shotgun in my roommate's car all the time and it's always a mess."

"I let my son use the car and look at how he treats it." Dana crumpled an empty Oreos bag. "I don't get any respect from anybody. Did you hear the way that reporter talked to me?"

"Yeah, but I don't think he meant any harm. He's just trying to do his job."

"And what job would that be—corporate spy? I swear, everybody has their own agenda around here. They're never on the up and up about anything." Dana turned the Subaru toward the freeway.

"Gee, Dana, you seem kind of angry. Is there something going on here I should know about?"

"I'm sorry." Dana realized suddenly how she was talking to her new employee. "I should be more professional. And you should make up your own mind about things around here. I'm sure it's like every other corporate environment. It's just that it never used to be this way. We used to be like a big family, all pulling together."

"What way, Dana? When I interviewed a couple of weeks ago everybody seemed so enthusiastic, talking about the new owners and the atmosphere to grow in different directions."

"Yeah, well, that's what they say. But as you'll see after you've been in the corporate world for a while, what people *say* and what they *do* aren't always the same."

"You mean they don't walk their talk?" Nikki asked, using the corporate jargon she had picked up from her interning days. "I hate it when people aren't authentic."

"Well, get used to it. Just make sure it doesn't rub off on you. How do you feel about some Tex-Mex? There's a place at the next exit with fantastic margaritas."

Todd and Matt both decided on the special of the day, a savory beef stew with cornbread, and settled into the corner table by the window, as alone as they could be in a company cafeteria.

"I think Dana is going into self-destruct mode. Jeanne and I both saw it this morning, and I can tell you Jeanne is worried about it."

"How do you know? Has Jeanne said something to you?" Matt asked, hoping for some inside information.

"Yeah, well, yes and no. We've been talking privately about my background in the beauty products biz, which is where I think Jeanne would like to see the company go. I can tell you Dana's shortsightedness is right in Jeanne's line of fire."

"Then she better get out of the way," Matt said too quickly. "When we recruited you from that industry I knew Jeanne had already decided that's where she wanted to take this company. I'm not surprised Dana is threatened. She only knows the candle business."

"Yeah, wicks and sticks," Todd said derisively. "It's been good to this company, I admit it. There's just not enough growth potential, that's all. I'm sad that Dana can't see that."

"She's never been the big-picture type. She hates change of any sort, she's threatened by both of us, and she and Jeanne are headed on a collision course."

"That was my impression this morning." Todd crumbled more cornbread into his stew. "Some people are going to *have* to change and I don't know if the old gal has it in her."

"Meanwhile, I've got to train our new employee, Miss Perfect herself, and hope Dana doesn't poison her against me and the whole company first."

"Yummy." Dana licked the salt along the rim of her margarita glass. "I can only have one of these or I'm finished for the day. It reminds me of that Dorothy Parker quote: 'I love to have a martini—two at the very most. Three I'm under the table, four I'm under the host.'"

"I don't do well with alcohol," Nikki responded demurely to her boss's racy remark. "I don't even drink coffee. I guess I just don't need the stimulation."

"God, wait until you have kids! If I didn't have my coffee I'd never make it to work. And I shudder to think how I'd deal with all the backstabbers there."

"You keep implying things are pretty bad at the company, but that just hasn't been my experience, at least not yet. Matt introduced me to lots of people this morning and they all seemed really welcoming."

"New blood," Dana said offhandedly, cracking herself up. "In more ways than one." The margarita was having its desired effect.

"I don't quite know how to say this, but if the company is growing and changing, isn't that a good thing? Think of all the new opportunities that come with growth."

"Growth and change are not the same thing, sweetie. Don't kid yourself that they are. Maybe there will be opportunities for people like you, but management often uses change as a way to escort the old guard out. I'm no spring chicken, you know."

"Oh, Dana. You're a fountain of knowledge. Everybody told me that when I was interviewing. 'You'll have this great chance to work with both Matt *and* Dana,' they said. Don't you see how valuable you are to the company? People really admire your history there."

"Yeah, the living scrapbook. When was the last time you heard about a *scrapbook* being promoted?"

"They mean that affectionately! Your experience is vital to the company's new direction."

"New direction—bull! You've been here all of four hours and you know more about this so-called new direction than I do. They've already decided all this without so much as a howdy-do to me. You should have been in that meeting with Jeanne and Todd this morning. I don't think they're saving a place for me." She pulled a tissue from her purse.

"Dana, Dana. You're reading more into this than you should. Sometimes you have to trust that things are going to turn out all right rather than worry that they won't. You believe that, don't you?"

"Easy for you to say. You've got your whole career ahead of you. I'm like a leftover meal. We should finish and get out of here. You've barely touched your food. Do you want to take it home for dinner?"

Nikki realized she had eaten almost nothing. "No. I have to watch my weight. You know, I used to weigh 60 pounds more than I do now."

"No way! You're a rail."

"Wa-ay. Maybe now I am but I honestly have to watch it," Nikki pointed to the basket of tortilla chips sitting between them. "I used to eat a bag of those chips every night before I went to bed—sometimes two. Do you think I ride my bike to work in the cold for *fun*? It's my exercise."

"Nikki, I am shocked. I know a lot of women who struggle with their weight, but I would never take you for one of them."

"It's a little more complicated than that. I actually struggle with my relationship to food in general. Millions of people do, not just women."

"Well, thank you for telling me that, Nikki. It makes me realize that people aren't always as trouble-free as they might appear. I mean, we all have our little secrets, don't we?" Dana drained her margarita. "We'd better go. I forgot that I've still got a whole afternoon of humiliation to look forward to."

"Oh, Dana, you're too much. Why don't I drive? You've got a lot on your mind."

"Thanks, Nikki. You know, you're a great listener. Where did you get so wise? Or is that one of those little secrets I was talking about?"

If only you knew, Nikki thought. *If only you knew.*

"It's 2:00 PM. Do you know where your sales director is?" Peter Abrams asked the receptionist, with just a bit too much familiarity.

"He's finished with his lunch and in his office waiting for you. He told me to send you right up. It's up the stairs and to the right, next to the big beehive."

Peter bounded up the stairs, smiling at the oversize sculpture that served as the company's official mascot.

"Matt Parker, I presume," Peter called into the plush corner office, pantomiming a knock at the partially open door.

"No presumption at all. You must be the guy who's out to expose this whole place," Matt kidded. "Glad you decided to start with the biggest imposter of them all. Sorry I couldn't see you earlier. Lots going on here."

"I gather that. Tell me more."

"What I'm going to tell you is off the record for the moment, Peter. You'll hear the official version from our CEO tomorrow, but let me forewarn you that things may not be as rosy as she may paint them. Do we have an understanding?"

Peter's wariness showed through his half-smile.

"You know, Matt, maybe it's better if I start with the corporate spin, if you will, and then you and I can talk about what's not so rosy, as you say. I'm not comfortable going off the record just yet. Jeanne invited me here and I feel some loyalty to her."

"Hey, Peter, not a problem," Matt hurried to say, clamping his arm around Peter's shoulder. "We'll just pretend this meeting never happened, okay?"

"Yeah, Matt, let's pretend that."

See page 98 for reading group discussion questions for this chapter.

3

AS BEES IN
HONEY DROWN

JUST WHO WAS this Jeanne Rasmussen lady, anyway? Peter Abrams sat by his computer, a steaming cup of morning coffee nearby, and entered "jeanne rasmussen bee natural ceo" into the Google search engine. He had done the same thing at least 50 times, as if some magical power might somehow take pity on him and reveal that Jeanne Rasmussen was a convicted felon, a shoplifter, or at least had an illegal cable box. Alas, this morning was no different. The search yielded a scant 35 entries—mostly connected to the press announcement of her appointment as Bee Natural's CEO a few months earlier. It also found a couple of op-ed-like pieces she had written for one of the female executive magazines, and showed she had created some lists of the "Best Books for Single Parents" on Amazon.com. Beyond that, she remained an enigma to the reporter. She had to be the lowest-profile CEO ever. Peter was just going to have to use his best interviewing skills if he was going to be able to get inside the mind of *this* CEO.

"I'm sorry, Mr. Abrams," the receptionist said when Peter arrived at Bee Natural's headquarters. "You must think I have nothing better to do than give you bad news, but Jeanne is on the telephone dealing with an emergency. She definitely wants to see you, but it may be a couple of minutes or more."

"Hey, you're just doing your job. I'll be happy to wait. I'll take a look at your annual report again. But if she needs to reschedule, we can do that too."

"I'll let you know when she's free, okay? Oh, wait a minute. It looks like she just hung up. Let me see what she says."

"Take your time. In my profession, you have to get used to waiting."

"No need to because the wait is over. She says to send you right up. Her assistant will meet you on the fifth floor."

Jeanne Rasmussen appeared totally composed when Peter was ushered into her office, but he felt he should ask about her emergency.

"It's under control, but we may have to make this an abbreviated meeting," Jeanne said. "Most people here don't know that I'm a single mother. I just got off the phone with the woman who helps me take care of my little girl. She's got a high fever, so I'll run home after we finish and check on her. Sometimes a little of mom's TLC goes a long way."

"Honestly, we can do this another time. You do what you need to do."

"I think we're fine. Let's just keep on point. Do you want to ask me questions or should I just talk?"

"If you'll permit me to tape this, it will be easier for both of us. Just begin—I'm sure I'll have questions for you as you go along."

"That's fine. So let me start by saying that I don't want to be the subject of your story. I don't even want this company to be the subject. I think it will help people more if your story concentrated on the changes we're going through here. Organizational change is probably the biggest challenge any company faces, and if our experience can help people, then that would make me very happy."

"Well, when I originally called your PR director, I told her that would be the angle for my story," Peter said, taken a bit by surprise. "But I'll have to quote you for attribution, as well as people on your team. And I'll have to name the company. I hope that's not going to be a problem."

"No, not for me, but there are some people you'll be talking to who won't be as enthusiastic about changes here as I am. I'm not going to spend a lot of time talking about new products or new packaging. I was brought in here to do something more fundamental—to get buy-in for change from as many of our stakeholder groups as I can. I think the largest group is our employee base, so I have been focusing more on them than on anything else I do. At least for now."

"Frankly, I think that's refreshing. You alluded to some employees who may not be as welcoming of change as you think they need to be. Is that code for something?"

"Peter, I don't speak in code, so if I need to be blunt, I'll just tell you the greatest challenge for me as a manager is to deal with what I've noticed is a disturbing lack of trust in our workplace. That single missing element has the power to sabotage any change initiative I put in place here."

"If there are people I shouldn't speak to, I'll respect your wishes, Jeanne."

"No. I don't want to edit our story. It's a good one. You have full access to my management team, to our books, even to our customer base. I have complete confidence that while you write your story on our 'corporate evolution,' if you will, the people who need to change will do just that. I'm also prepared to lose a key employee or two if they feel they don't like where I'm taking them.

"We have all types of people here," Jeanne continued. "Some are new employees, some are lifers, a few will tell me anything they think I want to hear, and a few think they should have my job. There are some 'unholy alliances,' as I like to call them, in the mix too. I don't think it's that different in any company anywhere. But when outside stakeholders are beginning to notice some of the toxicity that a few of these people bring to work with them, then I have to make sure I put into place as many things as I can to facilitate a healthier workplace. I have no illusions that I can do it alone, and I had hoped you reporting accurately on the changes we're making here could inspire people to row in the same direction as I am."

"Wow, Jeanne. I like your candor, but you've caught me off guard a bit. I thought we'd be talking about bees all morning."

"We can talk about bees all you want. You know my dad was a beekeeper, right? I don't know if that fact is on the Internet or not, but it's true. That's why I lobbied so hard for this job—to honor him. I grew up in Texas and my dad kept bees as a way to bring in more income. It's amazing how much those little critters can produce. And they're quite instructional organizationally, too. We can learn a lot from the hive hierarchy, you know. But I'll let the rest of the team go into specifics about how we make and market our products. They're much more knowledgeable than I am on those fronts."

Peter reached over and turned off the recorder.

"I like how you think, Jeanne. Let's leave it at that for the time being, though I'll probably want a tour of the plant and some follow-up time with you after I've interviewed some of your staff. Why don't you go home and administer some of that TLC?"

"You know, Peter, I was thinking the very same thing."

Matt Parker perched his chin on the top of Nikki Cavanagh's cubicle, surreptitiously watching his new employee master the intricacies of the company's intranet. She jolted slightly as he broke the silence.

"Didn't mean to startle you, Nikki. It's almost lunchtime. Can I buy you a sandwich?"

"That would be nice, Matt. I don't know what they're cooking down there but it smells great. My stomach has been growling for the last hour. Do you want to go now?"

"I'm ready if you are. Actually, let's see if Dana can join us."

"Join you for what?" Dana handed Nikki a freshly minted copy of the latest org chart.

"I was hoping I could invite you and Nikki for lunch, Dana. You had her all to yourself yesterday and I felt kind of bad that I couldn't join you."

"Then we'll be happy to let you spend your budget on us today."

"Hey, this is on my own dime. I want us to try and bond as a team from the get-go."

"You're on, Matt. Thanks."

As they made their way toward the company cafeteria, Nikki asked about the slightly sweet aroma wafting through the offices.

"It's honey," Dana said. "Every day the cafeteria makes something out of the honey our bees produce. I think I saw on the intranet that they're making honey-and-ginger cake today. It's one of the little side benefits that everybody takes for granted now."

"You mean you actually have bees on site?"

"Not in this building, but we think it's important that we don't forget our roots," Matt answered. "We hardly produce any of our own beeswax since we've grown so much, but we do have a small beekeeping staff just to 'keep us honest,' so to speak. Most people keep bees to produce honey, but for us it's about the wax. It's generally considered to be the oldest and purest substance on the planet."

"Yeah, and for years we were giving the honey away to local shelters and orphanages," Dana said, then ordered a crabmeat sandwich. "When we started to grow, we had to find other vendors to supplement our own wax. People sort of forgot about the honey the bees had been producing."

"Actually, it was Dana who suggested that we bottle the honey our own bees produce and give it to customers as a thank-you for their business," Matt said. "And Dana has always talked about never forgetting that our products come from the hive. I believe it was even Dana's idea, when we moved to these new offices with a cafeteria, that we have a honey-based menu item every day. I think it's a nice tradition."

"I guess I'd forgotten about all that. It was so long ago," Dana said. "Thank you Matt for reminding me."

"Nikki, Dana is responsible for so many good things this company has implemented over the years. She's too humble to admit to the impact she's had around here."

"Gosh, Matt, did you take a sweet pill or something?" Dana asked. "That's so nice of you to say all that. Nikki and I were talking just yesterday about how companies often struggle with balancing their need to change while still honoring their history. Weren't we, Nikki?"

"She's right. But you're right, too, Matt, that Dana doesn't realize how much she's respected here. Several people have already told me that. It's sad that so many people don't hear of their impact on a company until after they've left it."

God, I sound like such a suck-up, Nikki thought, though she was being totally sincere.

"Well, she'd be hard to replace, that's for sure." Matt made his way to a corner table overlooking the Japanese-style garden the company provided for its employees.

"Maybe I should be paying for this meal!" Dana said. "This flattery is good for the ego. And I need it, too, because we have family therapy this afternoon and it will be like an assault on Fort Dana. Could you both come and give me moral support?"

Matt and Nikki looked at each other before Nikki answered.

"Just go in and see if you can listen without feeling attacked. I'm sure nobody in your family means any harm. It's just part of any family dynamic."

"You know, Nikki, you sound so grounded for someone so young," Dana said. "If anybody is humble around here, I would say it's you, not me."

As Nikki finished her sandwich she said, "My mother sent me a refrigerator magnet that I see every time I sneak some Ben and Jerry's from the freezer. It says, 'Humility is not about thinking less of yourself. It's about thinking of yourself *less.*' I know these things probably sound like clichés to some people, but there's often a lot of truth in them. I guess that's why they become clichés."

"I agree with Dana," Matt said. "You seem almost too good to be true. We don't normally see people your age so mature.

I suspect you're going to have your own impact on this company if you can stay focused on the good things about it."

"Well, this probably sounds corny, but I believe people make their own reality, Matt. I guess the other cliché that I always remember is that one about the fundamental difference in people being how they see that proverbial glass of water—either half full or half empty. I see it as overflowing."

"How refreshing, Nikki." Dana beamed. "You remind me of the early days in my career. I just wish I could recapture some of that youthful exuberance again. Someday maybe you'll tell me your secret."

Maybe I will, Nikki thought. *Maybe I will.*

Dana had cagily scheduled her follow-up meeting with Todd Ramos for just prior to when she needed to leave for family therapy. She'd had root canals that were more pleasant than she expected this meeting to be.

As she approached Todd's office, she heard him talking on the phone.

"Mom, I told you. I'm really sorry but I just can't get out there for the holidays this year. This company is going through all kinds of changes. I told you last week they want me to come up with a new line of skin-care products. I'm up to my eyeballs in researching new vendors, and I don't have any help. Now I'm late for a meeting, so let me go. Tell Aunt Juana hello. Love you, Mom."

"Wasn't that just so sweet it makes my teeth ache?" Dana pulled up a chair. "It looks like we're starting a new business. I just think it might be nice if I knew about it before your mother. Doesn't my seniority count for anything around here?"

"Dana, I think we both heard yesterday that Jeanne has been given marching orders by the new owners to dramatically improve results. Come on, you must have suspected when they hired me we were probably going to start a personal care line. That's my background after all."

"Well, yes, I probably should have put two and two together. But I really think you could have kept me in the loop."

"I know, and I apologize, Dana. When you see the projections I've done for Jeanne you're going to be blown away. We can get this company past the $75 million mark in under two years with this new line of products."

"You have done sales projections?" Her fists clenched. "Without Matt knowing a thing? I find that totally unprofessional."

"Jeanne wanted this information to be carefully managed. You heard what she said about Matt yesterday. I built the projections based on what I know about the personal care industry. It's huge. And for the environmentalists out there, the bee connection is killer."

"What if we do get to be a $75 million company in two years? We're going to have to hire a lot more people. Do you realize how hard it is to find good employees here, particularly in the winter when people literally flee? I just don't think you've thought this through."

Todd waited a moment before springing his latest idea on Dana.

"Um, maybe we'll just have to move the company," he said offhandedly. "We're pretty remote up here, and I've heard you complain yourself about how difficult it is to fly to see our key customers. The company is changing, Dana. You have to realize that."

"Maybe *you* should realize that I have a family and that, while we have our problems, we love it here. And maybe *you* should realize that I have knocked myself out for this company. I am not going to be thrown out with the bathwater because someone like you wants to further his career."

Dana had the presence of mind to notice her whole body was shaking, but she had more to say. "We've got a board of directors meeting next week, and I am going to be as vocal as I need to be. You can talk all you want about your new line of products; that's your job. When it comes to moving the company, that's crossing the line and I will certainly say so. And Todd, let me also say that I don't like your tactics one bit. You say you have Jeanne's blessing, and if that's the case, I'm very disappointed in her. You can quote me, which you probably will. I'm now going to deal with some family issues. I heard you on the phone with your mom. I hope you're a better son than you are a coworker."

See page 99 for reading group discussion questions for this chapter.

4

LOOSE CANNONS

....

THIS DOESN'T SEEM *like a bad job at all,* Nikki Cavanagh thought as she prepared to have lunch with Bee Natural's CEO. *It's only Wednesday and I've already had three meals courtesy of management.*

An e-mail from Jeanne Rasmussen's assistant had summoned Nikki to the CEO's office at noon exactly for Jeanne's regular lunch with new employees. As she arrived at the assistant's cube, she was told Jeanne was expecting her.

"Do you want me to announce you?" he asked. "I'll be happy to."

"No, I'm fine introducing myself. This is a nice gesture— to have lunch with new employees."

"Yeah, and you're solo this time. You get her all to yourself."

As Nikki entered the expansive corner office overlooking the Japanese garden, Jeanne's back was to the door. She seemed to be intently studying a document on the intranet.

"Excuse me. I'm Nikki Cavanagh. I'm here for lunch."

Jeanne, obviously startled, whirled around a bit too fast, sending her left earring skidding across the pile of papers on her desk.

"Damn! I hate it when that happens." She quickly retrieved the errant jewelry. "I'm Jeanne Rasmussen, corporate klutz."

"So nice to meet you, Mrs. Rasmussen. This is very kind of you. I appreciate the opportunity to get to know you a bit."

Oh, my God. I must sound like a complete goon, Nikki thought. *She's going to think I'm from the sticks.*

"Call me Jeanne, please. Mrs. Rasmussen is my mother. And the pleasure is all mine. I really enjoy meeting our newest employees. You learn so much, if you're willing to listen. It's actually one of the highlights of my week. Since it's just the two of us today, I had a couple of salads and some juice sent up. We'll have more privacy that way."

"Don't tell me," Nikki said. "Honey mustard dressing."

Jeanne winked conspiratorially. "So you've heard about our little culinary tradition already."

"Yes, Matt told me yesterday that it was Dana's idea originally. I think it's a nice tradition."

"It was Dana's idea? I didn't know that." Jeanne made a quick note on her legal pad.

"I'm happy to be working for both of them. It seems they both have had a big impact on the company. Particularly Dana, since she's been here so long."

Was that a slam? Did it make Dana seem like a dinosaur?

As they moved to the marble-topped table Jeanne used for meeting with her department managers, Nikki noticed a striking photograph of a shirtless man surrounded by a swarm of bees.

"Jeanne, wow! That's a famous photograph. Does it have something to do with the company?"

"Oh, you recognize it? That is a photo of my father at our farm in Texas. He was a beekeeper."

"Cool!" Nikki said. "I've seen it reproduced in several of my photography books, and even on postcards. I always found it kind of disturbing, to tell you the absolute truth."

Now I've gone too far, she thought.

"Oh, me too. But he never got stung once in all his years working with bees, believe it or not. He always said he was too mean to get stung. It sounds like you know a little something about photography."

"Emphasis on little," Nikki said. "I took a course in school and totally got into it. I even had a basic darkroom that my dad built for me. After a couple of group shows in Providence, I realized soon enough that I just didn't have the eye for it, compared to the other students. But I'll always be interested in it."

"You know, we do new catalogs all the time here, and we always mix product shots with photos of the bees and the hives. Maybe you'd like to try your hand at some."

"Well," Nikki said, "I usually do black and white, but I guess I could *try* black and yellow."

Jeanne chuckled. "We're going to like having you around here. Bon appetit."

The lunch turned out to be more enjoyable than Nikki had even hoped. Jeanne was personable, interesting, even charming. When she started a gentle press for inside information on troop morale, however, Nikki felt a bit compromised.

"Jeanne, you're really easy to talk to, but I have only been here three days. My take on things is not very valid."

"But it is," Jeanne said. "A company needs feedback from everyone, and often the newest employees can give the best assessment of how things stand."

Oh boy, how much can she really take? Can I be completely honest with her? As Jack Nicholson said in A Few Good Men, *can she handle the truth?*

"Well, then, I hope I can be totally frank. I think there might be people here, not to name names, who are somewhat worried about what the new owners are going to do with the company."

"How do *you* feel, Nikki?"

"I guess I'm here because I like the respect the company shows for its roots and its values. Everybody seems really committed and involved in the business. I don't have a lot of experience in the corporate world, but at the company I just interned for, people joked the president didn't even know the price of the products we sold."

"Ouch! I'd probably have trouble writing a proper order myself. But that's not what I'm here for. There is a mandate from our parent company to change some of the corporate culture around here. I have a feeling people like you, Nikki, are going to help make that happen."

"I have to say, change has never felt as scary to me as it does to some people. My mom always says, 'With change comes opportunity.' And that's been my general experience."

"Well, just keep that attitude and there *will* be opportunities for you. I'll make sure of that."

Dana's restlessness during the night caused her husband to check in to their guestroom. Following the altercation with Todd, her son's hurled accusations during family therapy ("You don't have room for anyone in your life but you!") hurt Dana all the more. At least her insomnia allowed her to get to work early, for once. She couldn't wait to e-mail Matt.

Todd is up to something, she pounded furiously on her computer keyboard. *We need to confront him together. He's decided I'm the villain in this piece but he may listen to his buddy. Call me first thing when you get in.*

Not five minutes passed before the phone rang.

"Dana, you can't have another fight with Todd. I'll talk to him and see where he's coming from."

"So he told you? I knew he would. He probably told Jeanne too. I'm beginning to wonder if there's a conspiracy around here."

"Don't be so dramatic, Dana. I'll set up a meeting with the three of us after lunch. Maybe that will give you time to cool down."

"Well, make it 1:30 because I'm scheduled to talk to that reporter at 2:00. Just what I need."

Todd agreed to the afternoon meeting and was waiting for them with yet more designs for new packaging.

"So, is this the posse come to get me?" he asked in the most upbeat manner possible. "I have all kinds of things to show you."

"Save it for the staff meeting, Todd," Dana said briskly.

"Dana, just cool your heels for a minute," Matt said, supporting Todd. "He has let me in on a number of new initiatives he's working on and I think they show a lot of insight into where the company needs to go."

"So you *are* in this together? I might have known. Is Jeanne in on it too? Never mind—I'll ask her myself. That staff meeting tomorrow ought to be a barrel of laughs."

"Dana, you're overreacting," Matt said. "What exactly is so scary to you lately?"

"Just what I need—more taunts," Dana replied, noticing the self-satisfied grin creeping across Todd's face. "And what are you acting so smug about?"

"Nothing, Dana. I was just thinking of how much my mom was going to enjoy those flowers I sent her after our chat last night."

"Oh, aren't you the devoted son after all?" Dana said, dripping sarcasm.

On the way to her meeting with Peter Abrams, Dana stopped by the ladies' room to splash water on her face and attempt to regain her composure. The effects of her nearly sleepless night were readily apparent from the deep circles under her eyes. She had never felt so old.

When she got to her office, Peter and Nikki were already engaged in what appeared to be lively banter.

"Oh, hi Dana," Nikki said, rising from one of the guest chairs. "Peter was a bit early and you were in your meeting, so I went down and collected him."

"Early again, eh Peter?" Dana teased.

"Yeah, I was born two months premature and I've been early ever since. Nikki's been singing your praises, Dana, and telling me more about bees than I ever wanted to know."

"Well, I'm glad *somebody* has been saying nice things about me." Dana took her seat. "She knows a lot about human nature too. Both Matt and I think she's wise beyond her years."

"Dana, you're too kind," Nikki said, blushing. "I just read a lot of self-help books and they seem to apply to the workplace too."

"Then why don't you stay and listen in on our 'interview.' You don't mind, do you, Dana?"

"You read my mind, Peter. I think she offers a fresh perspective, which is definitely needed in my frame of mind."

"Is something wrong?" Nikki was genuinely concerned.

"I just feel a little weird putting a positive spin on things for a reporter when I feel the company is going through a very challenging time. I'm not sure our customers need to read about it."

"Dana, one of your colleagues alluded to the same thing," Peter said. "I'm not here to tell the corporate story or put a spin on anything. I'm interested in facts, and my readers can be helped by learning how a company they know and respect is reinventing itself. A lot of companies are having to do that these days."

"Reinvention is one thing, but an outright rejection of corporate values is another," Dana said. "If our parent company wants growth through new products, I can live with that. But some of the new hires here, and I certainly don't mean Nikki, seem bent on trashing the things people respect about us, and trashing some of the people too."

Dana looked out the window for an instant, contemplated what she was about to say, and then stared directly into Peter Abrams's eyes.

"Just yesterday I heard *thirdhand* that there is a plan afoot, that I want no part of, to move this company to another state!"

Nikki flinched. "Oh, Dana. That would be terrible."

"Wow! That's big news," Peter said. "You're one of the biggest employers in this part of the state. You know I'm going to have to report this."

"Go ahead," Dana said, almost as a challenge. "Maybe that will send a message to our new owners. Maybe they'll have to do some damage control. Maybe the PR people will have something to do for once—other than talk about bees!"

Oh, my God, Peter thought. *A loose cannon—every reporter's dream.*

Oh, my God, Nikki thought. *She's out of control. We've got to help her.*

See page 99 for reading group discussion questions for this chapter.

5

REIMAGINING THE FUTURE

THE STAFF MEETING was nearly half over and Dana had taken less than a page of notes. The CFO was recovering from a skiing accident, so it was just Jeanne, Matt, and Dana—for the moment at least.

I guess Jeanne is saving Todd for last so he can bowl everybody over with his new packaging designs, she thought. *Or maybe he's too worried about my reactions to them to actually show up.*

Matt was finishing his report on the focus group planning but Dana heard almost none of it. She allowed herself to recall for a moment the phone call she had received from Nikki at home the previous evening.

"Dana, I hope you don't mind me calling you, but I've been thinking about our meeting with Peter Abrams this afternoon," Nikki had said after a few pleasantries. "I walked out to the parking lot with him and convinced him to keep that news about moving the company off the record, for the time being at least. I'm not sure Jeanne would want to read it in the papers until she makes an announcement. Plus, it didn't sound totally confirmed anyway."

"Thanks, Nikki. Really, thank you. I guess I was a bit over the top. It's just that I am sick of being left out of the decision-making process around there."

"You know, I work for you and that puts me in an awkward position. But I think you're a wonderful person so I have to ask what you are so frightened about. Have you asked yourself that question?"

"Of course I have, but I don't think I'm quite ready to face the answer. At least that's what our therapist says."

"Oh, you talk about stuff that goes on at the company with your family therapist?"

"Sure, why not? It's all relative—no pun intended. I feel like you and him are about the only ones I can trust to be completely honest with. I guess I am worried I just won't be able to cut it in a different industry, and I'm not sure at my age I still have the stamina to deal with all the pressure to perform by our new parent company. More than anything, I don't feel like I'm getting any reassurance that everything is going to be all right. In fact, all the signs point in the opposite direction. Am I being silly?"

"I think it's totally understandable. I'm no sage, but I've known a lot of very competent people who have felt threatened when they had to learn something new. It's human nature.

But my mother always used to say, 'Change your thinking, change your life.' I know you're probably fed up with all my clichés, but I really believe in this one."

"What did she mean, do you think?" Dana asked with genuine interest.

"Well, we use our thoughts to process information. I'm also no psychiatrist, but it seems to me we can either think that something that happens to us is going to have a negative effect on us or a positive one. It's totally up to our thinking patterns, which then control how we respond. I told you the other day I just prefer to think that something positive is going to happen, and guess what? I'm usually right."

"That's easy for you to say because you haven't had a lifetime of bad stuff happen to you," Dana said, not at all convinced. "You develop a way of thinking based on things that happen to you."

"I just don't agree. I think it's the opposite. I believe our thoughts control more things than we know. I'd rather be a friend to my thoughts than a prisoner of them. We choose those tapes we play in our heads every day. I prefer to ignore the ones that say, 'I'm a bad person and I deserve the bad things that happen to me.' When I see you tomorrow I'm going to give you a book that has really helped me understand all this better."

"You know," Dana said, "you're actually making sense, even though a lot of this self-help stuff is pure baloney."

"A lot of it is bad self-help, that's for sure. I prefer to think of it as self-improvement. Promise me you'll read the book and see if it doesn't make you feel better about what's going on both at work and with your family. I won't push it on you, but honest to God it helped me a lot."

"You've got a deal. Now let me go finish that fight with my son. He absolutely refuses to take his SAT because he wants to be a songwriter. I just know he's going to end up working in a mailroom somewhere."

"Or maybe he'll win a Grammy, Dana. Think of that possibility too."

Maybe he'll win a Grammy, Dana thought, feeling a little better about things just as Todd walked into the conference room carrying an oversize cardboard box and snapping her right out of her own private reverie.

"Oh, perfect timing, Todd," Jeanne said, making room at the table.

Change Your Thinking, Change Your Life, Dana wrote at the top of her notepad. She was going to have to write it a lot, she thought.

"We've only got a few minutes left," Jeanne said, "but I wanted to give you all a preview of Todd's presentation to the board on Monday. He's done a lot of work in a very short time."

Here we go, Dana thought. *I'm going to have to keep my mouth shut. Change your thinking, change your life.*

Todd opened the box and, to everyone except Jeanne's surprise, began displaying samples of an entire new product line: a smooth beeswax-based lip balm; a moisturizing creme with lanolin, lavender, and beeswax; a beeswax and olive oil hand salve; a creamy foot lotion with beeswax and cloves; a tangerine peel and beeswax facial scrub—even a lime and beeswax cuticle creme. The room began to fill with tantalizing new scents.

"These are just a few of the new products I'm going to propose that we put into production," Todd said. "Ultimately, I'd like to do a baby line and even a pet line—all natural and 99 percent pure. I've lined up the manufacturing and they're being tested for the Consumer Products Commission and the FDA right now. We can outsource most of the production and launch the whole line at the spring gift show in New York."

"Todd, this is almost unbelievably quick work," Jeanne said. "The packaging is wonderful too. We probably should wait for the official approval from the board on Monday, but I have to tell you that I am totally behind this. What do the rest of you think?"

For once, Dana was almost speechless. She reached across the table for the tangerine face scrub. "This stuff smells fabulous. It almost makes me want to eat some. I can hardly believe you've done all this under the radar. I honestly had no idea."

"I wanted to keep this fairly low-key," Jeanne said. "There's a lot of competition in the personal care industry and I wanted to have as fully realized a presentation for the board as possible. Matt, what's your take?"

"I'm all for it, Jeanne. I think our sales force is going to be totally energized. They've been wanting a more diversified product line. I just hope we can fulfill easily because I wouldn't want to disappoint our customers. And I hope we can include these in the focus group studies. I admit I am kind of flabbergasted too—but in a good way."

"That's the word, all right," Dana said. "We're going to have to be careful how we communicate all this to our customers, but I guess that's part of my job. And I want to make sure that we don't lose track of our core candle business. It's been good to us."

"I said that just the other day," Todd said. "But the customers I've talked to absolutely love this company. If we manage this product launch well I predict they'll be thrilled that we have more for them."

"What about the packaging, Todd?" Dana wanted to know. "It has to be 100 percent recyclable. Our customers expect no less from us."

"Gotcha covered," Todd said. "I've even had them designed so we can use just two inks on the labels—soy based and fully biodegradable."

"Then the only other thing on my wish list is a trial size so we can give some to key customers and then make up travel cases with a variety of related products so people are more likely to try more than just one," Dana said.

"That is an absolutely brilliant idea, Dana," Jeanne said. "I love the energy that has developed in this room and on this team around this new direction. I think we've come a long way in a very short time. I feel the board will be easy to convince. They have to approve the funding, that's all."

Well, he did it all right, and this may be the lifeblood this company needs, Dana thought. *I just wish I trusted these people more.*

Nikki noticed immediately that Dana's spirits had brightened. She even thought she heard Dana whistling.

"I take it the meeting went well?" Nikki asked a bit cautiously. She wasn't used to this kind of response from Dana.

"That was a terrific meeting, and Jeanne even threw a little compliment my way. I worked hard to be as open minded as possible, and it seemed to work. I think I want to meet your mother."

"Oh, really? So you changed your thinking? Overnight? That's pretty fast."

"Maybe I *have* brought on some of my own problems here." Dana carefully weighed her words. "I still think people could be much better communicators about some of the new initiatives. That's all I want—to be part of the solution rather than the problem."

"Some people aren't the world's best communicators," Nikki said, "even though their intentions are good. Nobody's perfect. I'm glad you gave it a shot."

"Well, it was a good first attempt at least. I think I may need to work on the trust issue some more, and I'd like to see how these changes are going to improve *my* life, but overall I feel good about where we're headed—for the first time in a while. You know, I think you are an amazing person, especially for someone so young. Maybe *you* should be running this company." Dana laughed at the possibility.

"Dana, I'm going to tell you a little story. It may seem a bit convoluted, but it's got a point. Bear with me."

"Oh, goodie. I love story time." Dana clapped her hands like a schoolgirl.

"At my interning job last summer, I worked for a guy who was notoriously bad with technology," Nikki began. "Greg was a nice man, but anytime he had a problem with his laptop, his cell phone, the fax machine, even the copier, he would call me in to help him out. I got kind of sick of it, but I considered it part of my job."

"That's funny," Dana interrupted. "I'm a technophobe too, and my husband is a computer technician. I empathize already."

"Anyway, one day the company announced it was changing its e-mail software because another package had some meeting-planning features that were supposed to make us all more productive. My boss raged about it for nearly a week, refused to go to training after they installed the new software, and generally made my life miserable asking me about its fine points over and over.

"One day a buddy of his in Finance e-mailed him a copy of a confidential memo the president had sent him—as an attachment to the e-mail. Greg clicked on the attachment, didn't like what he read, and wrote a short but nasty response. He hit 'Send' just a tad too quickly. His reply went directly to the president's in-box."

"Oh, my God!" Dana said. "How bad was it? That kind of thing usually happens to me. Did he get canned?"

"It was pretty bad. Greg didn't call the president an outright liar but he did *imply* he wasn't being completely truthful in his memo."

"So go on. I'm dying to hear how this turned out."

"Well, he frantically calls me into his office to see if I can retrieve the e-mail, which of course I can't. So we phone the IT department and ask for their help. They say, 'Too bad, it's already been delivered to the president.' Greg, expecting the worst, phones his friend in Finance to say goodbye and starts packing up his office. The president waited nearly two hours to respond, but finally Greg called me back in to read it to him. He couldn't bear to do it himself. He truly expected to get the axe."

"And?"

"The message read, 'Hi Greg. I have a feeling you didn't mean to send this to me. But it does indicate that maybe our new e-mail software is not as easy to use as they promised it would be. Do you think the company needs more training on it?'"

"Amazing," said Dana. "What is that man's name and address? I wouldn't mind working for him."

"It *was* a pretty classy thing to do. Greg told him that perhaps some people *would* like more training in general and that he would spearhead a campaign to survey the employees about their training needs. Since I left there he's become the head of training and told me last week when I saw him at one of my meetings how much he's enjoying it. All because they *changed* e-mail packages."

"That is a fantastic story. So I guess you're trying to convince me that out of difficulty comes opportunity, right?"

"Well, that's the simplistic version. But it *is* my prediction for you, too." She reached into her backpack and pulled out a well-worn book with a bright yellow cover.

"This is what I was talking about on the phone last night, Dana. My oldest friend in the world gave it to me. This is my travel copy, so it's pretty beat up. I have another on my nightstand that I read almost every night. Here, this is your copy. It sounds like you're ready for it."

See page 100 for reading group discussion questions for this chapter.

6

FEELIN'
GROOVY

GETTING TO WORK early had at least one unexpected side benefit for Dana: plentiful parking. She had had another night with little sleep, but this time it was her own choice. The book Nikki loaned her engaged her right away; she stayed up until past 2:00 reading several chapters. Maybe Nikki was right. Maybe she *was* ready for it.

Its main point was far more complex than just "Change your thinking, change your life." It was a carefully reasoned near-manifesto for a less threatening, cognitive approach to behavior. By the time she went to bed, she had completed several of the self-assessments and turned down the corners of more than a few pages that particularly resonated with her. The author was a doctor but wrote in a gentle, nonjudgmental way. She brought it with her to work and planned to read more at lunch. *Maybe it would even help in family therapy,* she thought.

As she checked her makeup in the rearview mirror of the Subaru, the oldies station she and her son both enjoyed queued up one of Simon and Garfunkel's best—this time going out to Melissa from her coworkers at Denny's:

Slow down, you move too fast.
You've got to make the morning last.
Just kickin' down the cobblestones,
Looking for fun and feelin' groovy.

Dana realized for the first time in a while that she was feeling pretty "groovy" herself. She could hardly wait to share her enthusiasm with Nikki.

"Wow, Dana. You're in early," a rakish Matt Parker said as he passed her office. "Insomnia again?"

"No, Matt. I'm just enjoying a new book I've been reading. I was up half the night. Nikki loaned it to me."

Almost as if on cue, Nikki popped her head in, said "Good morning," and started shedding the layers of clothing she had to wear as a bicyclist in wintry New England. She began settling into her cube, where Matt and Dana joined her.

"Nikki, you bike to work in weather like this?" asked Matt. "You are almost *too* perfect."

"Oh, believe me, I have my faults—and my secrets too." Nikki unwound her polar-fleece scarf and gave Dana a private wink. "It's good for me, though I do need some hot chocolate. Can I get either of you something?"

"You can get me a speed-reading course," Dana joked. "I was up 'til all hours reading that book you loaned me."

"*Gave* you, Dana. I told you I have another copy. It's not the first one I've given away. I take it you're liking it?"

"I have to say I was skeptical at first," Dana said. "Those self-help books are usually too upbeat and simplistic for me. But this one is rooted in science and medicine, and it just makes a lot of sense. After the first two chapters I started to take a hard look at how I process things that happen to me. And I remembered what you said about not allowing your thoughts to imprison you."

"Dana, I'm so proud of you. You're giving it a shot," Nikki said. "Just keep in mind that a lot of it is easy to forget when you're in the middle of a difficult situation. The key to whether any new behavior strategy works for you is how you use it when dealing with stress."

"Oh, I totally agree. I was thinking on my way to work that maybe I would try to remember this stuff at our family counseling session tomorrow."

"You've got that again, Dana?" There was a hint of accusation in Matt's voice.

"Yes, we do. But notice I changed it so I don't have to take time off from work. We're going to talk about Chris's career—as a songwriter."

Nikki smiled knowingly. Her phone rang just as she finished packing away her cold-weather gear. The caller ID told her it was the company's CEO.

"Oh, good morning, Jeanne."

"Hi, Nikki. I was just wondering if you would ask Dana to give me a call when she gets in."

"She's already in. In fact, she's standing right here. Do you want to talk to her?"

"No, just ask her to come up to my office. I need about five minutes of her time."

"I'll tell her right now. Bye, Jeanne. And thanks again for lunch."

Dana drummed her fingers on the top of Nikki's computer monitor.

"What was that all about? She calls *you* to talk to me but then gives *you* the message? She must be on the warpath about something."

"Don't jump to conclusions," Nikki admonished. "She sounds like she's in a great mood. She said she just needs five minutes of your time."

"I know. My bad. When you get your hot chocolate could you bring me a half-full glass of water, please?"

Nikki and Matt both laughed at the reference to Dana's newfound optimism.

"Maybe I need to read that book," Matt said. "Seems like it's already helping you."

"Nikki, don't tell him what it is. Men shouldn't be as happy as women," Dana teased.

"Hey, that's not fair!" Matt said. "We can change our stripes sometimes too, you know."

"Easier said than done, Matt. I'm still wondering just how much it has helped me. This meeting with Jeanne ought to be a good test, don't you think? See you in a few."

Jeanne's assistant hadn't yet arrived so Dana casually walked into the CEO's office.

Change your thinking, change your life.

"Good morning, Jeanne. Nikki said you wanted to see me. What's up?"

"I would say it's your stock, frankly, Dana. I only wanted to tell you how impressed I was with you at the staff meeting yesterday. You asked some excellent questions and had a couple of great ideas. To be totally honest, Peter told me a bit about your meeting yesterday and I was worried I would have to give you a little pep talk before the board meeting. It seems like that won't be necessary now."

Dana blushed before responding.

"You know, Jeanne, that totally makes my day. I'm sorry about losing my cool with Peter. I heard something about moving the company and it made me worry that things were being decided without my input. You met my new assistant the other day for lunch, right? Candidly, she's enabling me to see things through a new employee's eyes and it's having a big impact on my thinking. She actually asked me yesterday what my fears were about what's going on with all the changes here. When I asked *myself,* I finally realized maybe I was afraid of not being able to make it here—that I would be exposed to you, the board, and the new owners. Nikki says that everyone has some level of fear and that it's how people deal with that fear that determines whether things will turn out well for them or poorly. She has told me several times that you have to trust that things will work out rather than worry yourself to death that they won't. I'm reading a new book that makes the point even further, using a medical and therapeutic framework."

"Well, I concur with Nikki. There have been times in my life when I have felt like a fraud, too. I think everyone does from time to time. That's what makes us stretch, to try new challenges. I have to say I was impressed by Nikki, too. She has a level of maturity that's rare these days. That's kind of you to give so much of the credit to a junior employee. Not everyone would."

"Well, she was a great hire and she has opened my eyes."

"I have to admit, Dana, that there *is* something to that rumor about moving the company. I haven't said anything to you because it certainly hasn't been decided, but that subject will probably come up at Monday's board meeting. I know that's a major issue with you, and I understand why. I just want to warn you that it is a possibility. It's not a done deal by any means, so let's keep it to ourselves for now."

"Thanks for telling me. It's always better to hear things officially. I guess I will just have to think about the options that would offer, *if* it happened. I want to say outright that I am solidly behind the success of this company, Jeanne. If I have said or done anything to make you think otherwise, then it comes from my own fears and I apologize. I can't believe I'm saying this, but I feel I have behaved rather selfishly lately. I am going to try and trust the team and grow with them and the company—*wherever* it is. I hope I can come to you whenever I think I need a little coaching on just how to make the biggest contribution here."

"You know my door is always open, Dana. What I really called you up here about was to ask if you need any help on your part of the presentation to the board on Monday?"

"No, I think I'm okay. I've got it written out in my head. My husband is giving up his Sunday afternoon football to help me get it into a decent PowerPoint slide show."

"Then I'm going to *trust* that everything will be topnotch. Feel free to call me at home if you need to. I'm in the book."

"You're on, Jeanne. But I'm involved with another book right now."

See page 101 for reading group discussion questions for this chapter.

7

REFRIGERATOR WISDOM

BOTH NIKKI CAVANAGH and her roommate, Barbara Morales, had been awakened early by the fury of the nor'easter that had blown into the city overnight. Winds of nearly 45 miles an hour rattled the windows throughout their loftlike apartment near the harbor, and the chill inside the apartment brutally reminded them that *Poor Richard's Almanac* had predicted they were in for a difficult winter. Nikki was not going to be biking anywhere today. She thought it would be a good morning to make a batch of her famous homemade granola.

"I can't believe we're out of honey," Nikki called to Barb, who was reading her e-mail across the enormous living-dining-kitchen space. "I'm working at Bee Natural and we're out of honey. How ironic is that?"

"I am pretty sure we have some." Barb brought her coffee mug into the kitchen for a refill. "Check behind that big box of oats in the cabinet next to the stove."

"Oh, yeah. Here it is. I didn't want to have to go to the store in weather like this just for honey."

"So how *is* Bee Natural anyway?" Barb asked. "You haven't talked much about it since your boss blew up at that business reporter the other day. Sounds like she is more than a little volatile. Did you hear anything more about moving the company, or was she just blowing smoke?"

"Dana means well. She was feeling threatened with all the changes going on there. Like a lot of people I guess. I didn't hear anything else about moving the company, but that meeting with the reporter scared me. I think Dana is actually a very good person, and some of the customers I talked to this week absolutely love her. The company needs her, that's for sure. I talked to her a couple of times during the week and gave her one of the books that has helped me a lot. She's reading it now and says she's actually seeing things in a different light. You know, 'Change your thinking, change your life.'"

"Oh, Nikki, you're sweet but sometimes I think you're way naïve." Barb sliced a bagel. "You can't live your life based on slogans you see on refrigerator magnets."

"Gee, thanks for your support." Nikki turned the oven on for the granola she was making. "Honestly, I have already seen a difference in her attitude. I know people have to practice new behavior over the long haul for it to make a significant difference in their lives, but I think it could be working with her already."

"Be careful, sweetie. People don't change their stripes overnight. Watch out for a trick!"

"Trick? You've been in the corporate world too long, Barb. I think her intentions are good, but she hasn't had much success recently with trusting people. She's got some family issues too. She needs to realize that much of the way something turns out has to do with how you approach the problem to begin with. I totally believe if you expect something to work out, usually it does. But people have to experience that themselves before they'll believe some therapist saying it in a book."

"I would agree with that—in general. But honestly, we're not talking here about somebody who's new on the scene, right? Didn't you tell me she's in her mid-forties?"

"Yeah, but it's never too late. I'm going to keep coaching her and we'll see what happens. I think people also mirror the behavior they see in people they like and admire."

"So you're mentoring *her*? Shouldn't it be the other way around?"

"Not necessarily," Nikki answered with some ambivalence. "I don't think it has to do so much with rank or position, but with how secure you feel in yourself. Dana's not there yet— but she might be soon. And I can learn a lot from her about marketing and customer relations. She really knows what she's doing in those areas. She just doesn't have a lot of confidence in herself right now."

Barb opened the refrigerator door to get some soymilk for her coffee. She couldn't help taking a swipe at another of the magnets Nikki had attached to it.

"So here's some more fridge wisdom: 'Let go and let God.' Have you told Dana where all these slogans come from?"

"You mean OA? Not yet. I might soon, but not everybody is as open to these 12-step programs as you might think, despite how helpful they could be. Besides, it's supposed to be *anonymous,* you know."

"But you told *me.* People can decide to out themselves if they choose, right?"

"Yeah, absolutely. I'll probably tell her, when the time comes." Nikki mixed the oats, wheat germ, and honey. "In fact, I'm thinking maybe I'll go over there tomorrow and help with the board presentation that she has to give on Monday. The weather sucks anyway, and I wouldn't mind a chance for a little reinforcement on some of the things she's reading in that book I gave her."

"Nikki, be careful," Barb warned. "This could backfire on you. I know your intentions are pure, but this is new stuff for her. She may need some time for it to sink in, *if* she decides she really wants to change. You said it earlier—she's threatened. That is a very scary place to be for most people. Maybe you should leave it alone. Some people get resentful when they feel like they're being forced to do something they're not ready for."

"I appreciate your advice, Barb, but I like this new company and I want to give it my all. People respect Dana, and if they see her changing it's likely they will be more accepting of new things too. If I can help the process, then I feel I have almost a duty."

"Nikki, you're brand new there. How much impact do you think an admin can have, anyway? I'm not putting you down, but just how realistic are you being?"

"You make a good point. I remember once when I was interning and the main receptionist went on maternity leave. People thought she was terrific and told her they could never replace her. Well, they did, with a temp. She was maybe even better, and people just went crazy for her. She had some ideas right off the bat for improving things around the company. Before you know it, the company changed a couple of policies that had been in place for years. It *can* happen."

"Yeah, it can. But you've got to be careful about how you deliver the message. You don't want people to think you're a corporate robot."

"That's the risk you have to take, Barb. Otherwise things never change, anywhere. I'm willing to take that risk, but I appreciate your point about delivering the message properly. I'll be a little more careful with how I deal with Dana. I don't want to push her, but I genuinely like her and want the best for her. I'm going to call her now. You don't think it's too early, do you?"

"I bet she didn't get much sleep either, so why not? She's probably beating her children right now anyway."

"You are *awful!* No granola for you. I'm going to call her."

The phone rang several times and just as the answering machine picked up, Dana came on the line.

"Chris, I'm sorry I hung up on you, but you know we have family counseling in an hour and I want you *home!*" she said. "After that stunt we talked about last night, this will be mostly about you anyway."

"Sorry, Dana, it's Nikki. I hope it's not too early."

"Oh, hi, Nikki. I thought it was my son. He spent the night with a friend and now doesn't want to come home for 'happy hour,' as I call it. I went to the trouble of rescheduling so it wouldn't interfere with work and now he doesn't want to go."

"Well, maybe you could skip a week. It's pretty raw out there anyway. Are you sure your therapist will even be in the office?

"I guess the weather might make him close it, particularly on a Saturday. I should call. I had to have a talk with Chris last night because I found out he had lied about his age and gotten a credit card off the Internet. His father told him he couldn't have supper, which I thought was too harsh, so we all had a fight about it. He ran off to his buddy's house and sulked while his father and I didn't speak for the rest of the evening. If there ever was a time when we *needed* family therapy, this is it. What am I going to do with him?"

All this came under the heading of "too much information" in Nikki's mind, but she pressed on anyway.

"Gee, Dana. I'm sorry. What did he buy with the credit card?"

"That's the funny thing. He didn't buy anything. He just wanted to show it off to his friends. I was more upset that he lied about his age, but I used that approach from the book and thought it through before I confronted him. We kind of laughed about it, actually, until I told his father what he had done, and, predictably he exploded. Those two have quite the relationship."

"You used the approach from the book, eh? That's good news. What was different about the outcome?"

"Well . . . he didn't throw it back in my face like he usually does—'If you guys would *get* me a credit card I wouldn't have to do it behind your back.' I think he also saw me taking his side against his father, and that brought us a little closer. He's still testing me, though, with this thing about staying over at his friend's house. I'm not going to be drawn into a big drama about it. I have learned my lesson."

Nikki smiled to herself as she mixed the sticky ingredients in the granola.

"That sounds great. I'm sure whatever happens will be what needs to happen. I was calling to see if you wanted me to come over tomorrow and help you with the presentation for the board on Monday? I am a PowerPoint goddess."

"Oh, Nikki, that would be great! My husband was going to help me and now we're fighting, so if you could do it that would really take the edge off. He can watch his football while the girls do high-tech for a couple of hours. You don't mind?"

"Dana, it's a mess outside. I wouldn't offer if I didn't want to help. I'll probably learn a lot in the process too, you know."

"I told Jeanne I had it all written in my head, so if you can just help me organize and shape it a bit, I will be eternally grateful."

"Eternity is a pretty long time," Nikki teased. "I'll be over around 1:00. Just have some hot chocolate for me, okay?" She added the last of the dried fruit and the maple syrup into the granola mixture.

"I'll light a fire in the den, too. See you tomorrow. Now let me call the therapist's office and see what's up with that," she said. "I'm sure my husband doesn't want to miss a chance to yell at me some more."

"Dana . . ." Nikki scolded.

"I know, I know. CYT-CYL. That's shorthand for you know what."

"That's better. SYT."

See page 102 for reading group discussion questions for this chapter.

8

NEW BEHAVIOR

"MOM! I'M GOING to be late for rehearsal unless you get a move on," Chris yelled from his upstairs bedroom. "You know, I'd be happy to drive myself if you don't feel like taking me. Or I could call Dylan and have him pick me up. He's got his *own* car."

Another dig, Dana thought. *He dug himself into this and got grounded. He can just dig himself out.*

Family therapy hadn't happened because of the terrible weather, but Dana, her husband, and Chris had held a family meeting the previous night that had gone fairly well, in Dana's mind at least. Though her husband remained in a punitive mood about Chris's "banking adventure," Dana convinced him to take away Chris's driving privileges for only a week, and to limit his computer usage to one hour each night. Of course, that meant she and her husband would be doing a lot more chauffeuring for a week, so who was actually getting punished?

"Go ahead and call Dylan then," Dana said, as Chris bounded down the stairs. "My new assistant is coming over in a few minutes, so Dylan can take you. Be sure to bundle up, though, and be home by 6:00. And don't tell your father."

"Thanks, Mom. You know Dylan also has his own cell phone."

"Don't push it, Mister Man. You're lucky we're letting you out of the house."

"Oh, Mom. What I did wasn't so bad. Nobody got hurt."

"What you did was fraud, Chris. That's a criminal offense. If the bank found out, they could press charges against you. Don't try to minimize it. I've told you about the consequences of lying."

"But you lie all the time."

"That's not true! I am almost always totally honest."

"No, you're not. I heard you just yesterday telling Dylan's mother you and Dad couldn't go to the movies with them because you had dinner plans. You didn't have any dinner plans."

"Oh, Chris. That's a social lie," Dana said. "Those don't count. We didn't want to get out in the middle of this storm, that's all."

"Why don't you admit you don't like his parents? They're too permissive for you guys."

"Chris, that's just not true. Sometimes these little social lies are necessary. They're just easier."

"They're still lies, aren't they?"

Dana hesitated before admitting defeat.

"Okay, you win. They're still lies and I am going to be more aware of them from now on. Thanks for pointing it out to me. I guess I'm a bigger offender than I thought. Now go upstairs and call Dylan."

The doorbell rang at the same time as the teakettle whistled. Dana thought for the first time about how Nikki was getting to her house. *I hope she's not frozen to death,* she thought.

Nikki looked like the Invisible Woman under all the scarves wrapped around her head. Dana happily welcomed her inside the toasty split-level house. "I'm so sorry. I should have come to pick you up. Your roommate brought you here, I hope."

"No, I took the bus. It was pretty easy, but I had to walk two blocks and that wind is biting."

"You are a tough cookie," Dana said. "I'm just making that hot chocolate I promised. The good news is I worked on the presentation this morning and it's virtually finished. I would welcome your input on the way it looks, but we can have a visit instead of working all afternoon. Take those shoes off and I'll get you some slippers. I'll get you a lap blanket too."

Nikki gradually peeled off all her insulation and sat down to slip her duck shoes off. "I don't think I've ever been so cold. I'm going to sit by the fireplace for a minute, Dana. I brought you some homemade granola. I think it's great you and PowerPoint got along."

"I've been making excuses for not using PowerPoint for years. I never thought I could do it before, but it's not so hard.

It's like making an outline and then letting the program turn it into a slide show."

"Well, like those self-help books, there's some really bad PowerPoint out there too. In my experience it's a bit overused."

"Speaking of that, I finished the book you gave me last night. We had a family meeting after dinner to talk about the credit card incident and I think it helped me to see things from a different perspective. I shudder to think what might have happened if I hadn't changed my thinking a little bit. I'm sure we would have had another major fight." Dana handed Nikki the cup of steaming hot chocolate.

"This is good news, Dana. I think people have to have some successes with new behavior before they commit to it for the long term. Sounds like you're on your way."

"Well, maybe. That meeting tomorrow could be a big challenge, though. Jeanne told me the board might be talking about some major changes ahead."

"Did you ever hear anymore about the company moving to another state?"

"I'm not supposed to talk about it, but I guess, like a number of things, it's a possibility. We discussed it in the family meeting too."

"And?"

"Believe it or not, both my husband and my son were open to the idea. My husband could do his computer consulting just about anywhere, and of course my son has visions of moving to Nashville. He's already written a song that he thinks Shania Twain should record. He's a dreamer like nobody I've ever seen."

"Nashville? Is that a possibility?"

"Who knows? It's all speculation at this point. If this new initiative is approved, there's no doubt we would have to hire people, and it might be easier to find them down South. Nashville is fairly central, it's a transportation hub so shipping would be faster, and I suspect the labor is cheaper overall. Plus, the weather has to be better than this." She waved a hand to the snowy landscape beyond the French doors and the deck.

"Dana, this is amazing. Just the other day I remember you being violently opposed to moving the company. You're not going to tell me all this came from reading that book, are you?"

"No, but that book *did* allow me to open my mind a little bit to other possibilities. And frankly, Nikki, seeing how you deal with change has been inspirational to me. My husband said in bed last night that he had noticed a major difference in how I process things, so we're back on better terms."

Chris almost tripped down the stairs in his excitement to get to band rehearsal. He clutched the sheet music under his arm to free both hands for carrying the cold-weather gear he would need.

"Dylan is waiting for me in the driveway, Mom. I promise I'll be home by 6:00."

"Hey, wait a minute. Don't be rude. I want you to meet my new colleague, Nicole Cavanagh. Nikki, this my wild son Chris."

"Oh, you're the Nikki my mom has been talking about," Chris said. "Nice to meet you. Are you moving with the company to Nashville too?"

"Chris, what a question!" Dana said, alarmed at Chris's directness. "I just said the company *might* be moving. I don't know if that will happen or not. I certainly don't know that it's going to be to Nashville."

"Pleased to meet you too, Chris," Nikki said. "In weather like this, I'm certainly open to the company moving elsewhere. But I've been there a grand total of five days. Finding my way to the ladies' room is still a challenge. I've come to help your mother with her presentation. It's going to be a very important meeting tomorrow."

"Nashville would be just fine with me. I'm sick of these winters too. But didn't you say you'd already finished that presentation, Mom? Or did you *lie* about that?" He smiled at both women. "Just kidding. See you later."

"What was that all about?" Nikki asked.

"He was grilling me earlier about the little white lies we all tell. He's just trying to distract me from the credit card thing. But I remembered the book and deferred the argument he would normally pick. I think I'm doing better. I do."

"You know," said Nikki, "the other day I said something about not liking people who aren't authentic. Those white lies are what keep people from being as authentic as they could be. In the program we talk about absolute honesty, so that's the way I operate, and I encourage it with everybody I meet."

Dana got up to put another log on the fire.

"Well, that's admirable, Nikki. I told Chris I would be more aware of it in the future. I hope to be able to use this new behavior in the meeting tomorrow. I suspect the rest of the team is going to be surprised. Would you mind taking a look at that presentation now? You might have to use your imagination for some of the graphics I haven't been able to master yet."

"Don't worry, Dana. Imagination is a *good* thing, as Martha Stewart would say."

See page 103 for reading group discussion questions for this chapter.

9

SHOW TIME

MATT PARKER ARRIVED early, as was his custom, but a re-
formed Dana followed him soon after. As Matt poured water
into the coffeemaker, Dana snuck up behind him.

"No, this is not an illusion, Matt," she said. "I changed
some of my morning routine to allow me to get in earlier. I
didn't want to have to rush to put the finishing touches on my
presentation. I think it looks good. Nikki helped me a little bit
yesterday, but mostly I mastered PowerPoint on my own.
Matt, I wanted to say that I know you've been covering for me
these past few weeks, and I appreciate it. Things are better at
home so I can devote more time to my work."

"Dana, we're on the same team. I appreciate you saying
that, and I'm happy for you if what you've said about your
family is true. I meant what I said earlier—maybe I need a
copy of that book too. It seems to have worked wonders."

"It wasn't only the book. I told Nikki that her upbeat attitude had a lot to do with my new thinking too. She made me

realize that as I was growing comfortable in my misery—I was making people around me just as miserable. That's not fair to anybody."

"That's a healthy self-evaluation," Matt said. "It takes a big person to admit something like that. So you mastered PowerPoint, did you? Ready to do a testimonial for Microsoft?"

Dana chuckled. "Not just yet, but I think you're all going to be impressed. I just hope the board is. I'm a little intimidated, to be totally truthful."

"Totally truthful is the only way to be," a red-cheeked Nikki Cavanagh said, out of breath from her morning commute. "Now get out of my way so I can make my tea. I am totally frozen."

"Get *her*," Matt said. "I guess she knows by now why this place is not the setting for any Tour de France events. Is this weather a little rough for you, princess?"

"Hey, leave her alone," said Dana. "She's getting good exercise and not polluting the environment. I admire her dedication, not to mention stamina."

"Oh, I was only kidding, Nikki. With all this sweetness and light around here I had to tease you a little bit."

Dana poured coffee for the two of them and asked Matt what he wanted in his. "How about some Skinny 'n Sweet?" she asked demurely, referring to the poisonous compound that Lily Tomlin feared she had put in her boss's coffee in the funniest workplace movie of all time, *9 to 5*. Nikki was too young to catch the joke, but Matt quickly grabbed the sugar out of Dana's hands.

"Oh, I see some things haven't changed, Dana. Your wicked sense of humor is still intact."

"Okay, you two. I've got work to do," Nikki said. "Let me know if you need any help before the meeting starts. And it might be a good idea to call Jeanne and offer some help to her."

"Nikki, you kill me," Matt said. "One of these days I am going to figure out just who you were in a previous life—Joan of Arc or Marie Curie?"

Todd Ramos waited just outside the conference room for Jeanne Rasmussen, the show-and-tell box of new products at his feet. Jeanne had impressed on him the importance of a solid presentation, and after much rehearsal he felt he was up to the task. As he checked his reflection in the window, the elevator doors opened, revealing Peter Abrams, the business reporter, who would be attending the meeting as an observer.

"Good morning, Todd. We're not *that* early, are we? Where is everybody?"

"Hey, Peter. I quit keeping tabs on people a long time ago. They know what time the meeting starts, but I'm surprised Jeanne isn't here yet. I'm sure Dana will be late, as usual."

"Wrong again, mister," Dana teased, coming out of the stairwell. "I've been here a good half hour already. I'm on my third cup of coffee. How are you, Peter? How's the story going?"

"Great, I think. They've given me an extra week, and you'll be getting a whole spread in the Business section."

"Todd, you've been filling in Peter on all your new product ideas, right? If you haven't actually seen them, Peter, you'll be blown away."

"Thanks, Dana," Todd replied cautiously. "Yes, Peter knows the general outline of what I've been working on, but that's all. I wanted to save the good stuff for the meeting. I knew he would be here covering it."

Dana turned to Peter. "You know about Todd's background in the personal care industry, right? Well, I haven't been giving him enough credit. The board should be blown away, too. At least that's my prediction. I think, with this new product line, we can substantially grow the business. We might even have to move the company."

Peter's astonishment was obvious.

"Dana, I have to say, you seem like a different person from the woman I talked to last week. Wasn't it you who told me that would happen over your stone-cold dead body, or something to that effect?"

"Sometimes you have to trust that things will work out for the best," Dana paraphrased her assistant. "Strangely enough, Nikki is the one most responsible for showing me the way. It's a pity junior employees are so seldom asked for their input in helping a company determine its future, or for giving the jaded among us a fresh new perspective. I give her full credit. And let me apologize to Todd in your presence for all the doubts I originally showed about this new direction. I just wasn't being open minded about it at all. I am so energized to be on this team again."

"If you don't mind going on the record, I would love to use some of your 'transformation' in my story," Peter said. "I think it could be inspiring to a lot of people who are feeling stuck. Are you comfortable with that?"

"I'm perfectly fine being quoted on this subject, though I'm certainly not an expert. I'm just trying to live it day to day."

"Dana, I had a feeling you would come around," Todd said. "You're too much of a pro not to."

"How about 'old hand'?" She smiled as Jeanne arrived to usher them all into the conference room.

"Okay, folks. It's show time."

The board meeting took the better part of the morning and, as expected, Todd was the star. His presentation was smooth and thoughtful, and he took board members along for the ride. Jeanne beamed throughout the meeting and even winked several times at Dana. Dana's own presentation paled in comparison, but she kept her nerves at bay and worked the computer like the pro Todd said she was. Matt was commanding in his knowledge of Bee Natural's customer base, and their CFO supported Todd's product plans with solid, credible numbers. Dana could hardly wait to tell Nikki the news.

"You're *not* going to believe what happened," Dana said, sailing past Nikki's cube into her own office. "Come in and I'll give you a synopsis. It was an amazing meeting."

"Just a sec, Dana. I want to finish this e-mail to my mom. She sent me a cute note with some more words of wisdom. I'll print it out and bring it in."

Dana took a moment to check her voicemail and e-mail, and was pleased to discover nothing urgent had come up during the morning. She sat quietly at her desk. For the first time in a while, she breathed—deeply. She felt the tension that had been building around this meeting subside.

Nikki arrived, blowing on her steaming tea.

"So what happened? Are we moving?"

"Yes and no. The board approved the launch of the new product line and wants to ramp up production right away. The CFO has already arranged a new line of credit with the bank, just in case, and they think we can have product samples by late March. It's going to be a push, but I think it's exciting. I have my assignments: Get feedback from our major customers and start looking for a satellite location to support the launch."

"Oh, my God, Dana, that is amazing! So we're staying here *and* opening a new office? That's great. Where do you start?"

"Well, I start with polling the customers, of course, but I guess I'll be doing a little geographic research."

"I think Nashville is in Tennessee," Nikki teased.

"You know, Nikki, I've apologized to everyone else today so I might as well do the same with you. If I in any way was dismissive of your 'clichés,' as you call them, I am sorry. I now realize how much truth they actually contain. It was your delivery of them that made an enormous difference. Not everyone is as gentle with this kind of 'challenge to change' as you have been. I'm not so sure I would have accepted the idea that with change comes opportunity if it came as an edict from on high."

"Everyone comes to an understanding of their own truth in their own time," Nikki said. "You don't owe me an apology for anything. I'm just glad I could help you. I saw you were hurting. I see other people suffering all the time, and I wish I could help them. They aren't as receptive to the message as you were. You were ready to hear it—and read it. I'm also glad it made a difference with your family. Chris is going to be so excited to hear how things turned out. You should probably call him."

"I will, but Nashville is not a certainty by any means. I have some major research to do. What's that you're holding? Is that the e-mail from your mother?"

"Yeah, she's at it again. She's cute, but sometimes. . . . You know, she's the one who gives me those refrigerator magnets that my roommate makes fun of. This latest is something she sent me in honor of my new job here. It's vintage Mom. Have a look."

Happiness is a choice.
Inspire yourself; others will follow.
Vanity is not a team sport.
Enthusiasm will take you 90 percent of the way.

See page 103 for reading group discussion questions based on this chapter.

CLEARED FOR TAKEOFF

FLIGHT 96—DELAYED.

Dana noticed on the departure board in the Orlando airport that bad weather in the Northeast was wreaking havoc even in sunny Florida. Dana's World Tour to scout satellite locations was damned hard work, indeed.

Oh boy, she thought, *this trip is going to challenge the new attitude I've cultivated. Could this winter be over—today?*

She didn't get the wake-up call she had arranged after finding her hotel alarm clock maddeningly impossible to set. Her cab driver had gotten lost on the "shortcut" to the airport that Dana agreed to let him try. Then, because she was flying to four cities in six days, which required the travel agent to issue five one-way tickets, airport security identified her for everything short of a strip search. *Does it get any worse than this? They should just make everybody fly naked.* She smiled at the image of passengers struggling with their seat belts in the nude.

After some major research and a poll of company employees, Dana was on a fact-finding mission to Orlando, Nashville, Memphis, and Winston-Salem. She had meetings set up with chambers of commerce in each of those growing cities, all of which were keen to attract new industry. Orlando had been somewhat of a disappointment, but perhaps her son's enthusiastic endorsement of Nashville had colored her thinking. It certainly wouldn't be her choice alone, anyway, but her evaluation of the strengths and weaknesses of each city would play an important role in the board's ultimate decision. Dana had told her husband on the phone from the hotel that she was finding the assignment one of the most interesting of her career. She also didn't mind when he told her that she had missed yet another brutal winter storm.

Pulling her wheelie behind her, Dana arrived at the gate just in time to witness a passenger screaming at the gate agent about the flight's delay.

"I am going to miss my meeting completely if we can't get out of here by noon!" the irate executive yelled. "This has happened three other times this month and you do nothing about it except blame the weather."

"Please calm down, sir," the airline employee said. "It's actually not going to be a problem. We'll be boarding momentarily."

"Yeah, but since you couldn't upgrade me I'll be sitting in the back with the rest of the cattle. I think I'm in the last row, right across from the bathroom. How pleasant for me," he said sarcastically.

"Then we'll be boarding first, won't we?" Dana said, attempting to calm the situation. "I'm one of the cows in the last row too."

The gate agent was correct. Boarding commenced soon after and Dana ended up sitting next to the still-fuming passenger. When he realized his luggage was too big to fit into the overhead, it set him off on a whole new diatribe.

"Stewardess, can you stow this in the crew's First Class cabin?" he asked. "It won't fit in these dinky overheads. Of course, I *normally* fly First Class."

"I'm sorry, sir, but if it doesn't fit we'll have to gate-check it for you. We've got a full flight this morning because the earlier one was cancelled."

"And whose problem was that—mine? I don't think so. Flying gets worse and worse every day. Now I'll have to wait for the luggage to be off-loaded. I'll definitely miss my meeting now," he said to everyone and no one at the same time. "What a day."

"Try putting it under your seat," Dana said soothingly. "You don't want to have them gate-check it."

"Where am I supposed to put my legs? I'm over six feet so it's already uncomfortable in these seats back here."

"Hey, put it under my seat." Dana moved her legs aside. "It's a short trip and I don't need much legroom."

He softened. "That's really nice of you. I'm going to buy you a cocktail. I'm Barry Johnston."

"I know. I saw it on your luggage tag. I don't mean to meddle, but all that *agita* is bad for your blood pressure."

He took off his suit jacket, folded it neatly, and carefully placed it in the overhead. He settled into his seat and patted Dana's hand.

"It is. I know it is, but service in this country has gone to hell, and if we just blindly accept that fact, then we deserve our next world of self-service. Soon they'll expect us to fly the planes ourselves. I just feel I have to stand up for the customer."

"You're preaching to the choir, baby," Dana responded, "but there are ways of taking that stand that are a little less aggressive, if you don't mind me saying so. You attract more flies with honey than with vinegar."

Barry smiled at the cliché and began to relax.

"You know," Dana continued, "I just got out of the taxi-cab ride from hell. The driver spoke almost no English and, worse, he didn't even know his way to the airport!"

"That happens all over the place now. Nobody speaks English."

"You know, Barry, there was a time in the not-too-distant past when I would have 'gone all off on his ass,' as my son would say. I didn't. I breathed deeply and just sat back. What could I really do about it anyway? I almost missed this flight, so I was actually a bit relieved when I saw it was delayed."

"I wish I could be that laid back," Barry said. "What's your name and where are you from—Mars, or the Taxi Defense League?"

Dana chuckled, they exchanged names and handshakes, and she continued. She was determined to make a sale today—even if the product was free.

"I've just been trying to look at how my attitude makes a difference in how my day turns out. It seems counterproductive to me to see the glass as perennially half-empty, to expect the worst. It has taken some work, some patient colleagues and family, and a lot of reading, but it *has* made a difference in my life. I'm much less stressed than I've ever been. And, you know, reducing stress can add years to your life."

The plane finally crept away from the gate onto an active runway. It looked as if they were not going to be so terribly late after all.

"You make good sense, Dana. How'd you get so smart? And why are you going to Nashville?"

"Well, it took a book and a very wise new employee to get me to change the way I look at things. I'm going to Nashville because part of my company may be moving there."

"So what's the book called?" Barry asked. "I probably should mention it to my former boss, who now runs our corporate university. We're always looking for good 'bibliotherapy,' as he calls it. He buys hundreds of copies of new business books all the time and sends them out to key managers around the world."

"It isn't a business book," Dana replied, "and I don't know that huge companies with corporate universities like you have are the best incubators for new ideas. Those kind of companies seem kind of set in their ways to me. That's why I work for this little company that's trying to grow and evolve."

"Every company is trying to grow and evolve. It doesn't matter if it's a $1 million company or $500 million. Large companies have brain trusts, too, you know, and we often have budgets for training that smaller companies don't have. So don't go all off on my ass, as your son would say, and *assume* we are too Jurassic Park to profit by the thinking that you have found so valuable." He laughed, though Dana could tell she had touched a nerve.

"Okay, mister. Maybe I *was* jumping to conclusions. I'll tell you the name of the book. But each workplace has its own way of getting things right, whether it's pouring beeswax candles, like we do, or something life-changing like making an artificial heart. I just can't imagine, though, that the change strategies I read about in that book would be embraced by a really large company. It's only a self-help book. Does your company give those out or ridicule them like I used to do?"

"Flight 96 is number one for takeoff," the purser announced. "We thank you for your business and your patience. We should be able to make up some of the time and get you into Nashville just a few minutes late. We'll keep you posted."

"Now, that's more like it," Barry said. "Communicating about a problem is maybe even more important than resolution of the problem itself. I just wish people understood that more. And to answer your question, we don't ridicule anything that has the word *help* in it. My former boss, the one who runs the corporate university, has given out everything from *Fish!* to *Jesus, CEO.*"

The plane taxied down the runway, shuddering as it took flight. Disney World and the other theme parks got smaller and smaller as the plane made its ascent.

"That's good to know," Dana said. "Soon you'll be able to buy me that cocktail. Too bad they don't serve margaritas—my all-time favorite."

"I'm happy to," Barry said. "You've totally made my day. But I'm a little disturbed that you think big companies are such dinosaurs we can't do anything innovative."

"That's not exactly what I meant, Barry. I just think it's important for companies to get things right. So many of these large companies have their fingers in so many pies they've lost track of just what it is they *need* to get right. Don't you agree?"

"Dana, you are a lovely woman, and I'm happy we met. However, I think you might be a bit naïve. Pouring your candles is important, I'm sure, but my company is one of the largest in the world, and we would welcome any kind of new way of motivating employees to get things right—self-help book or not. We wouldn't have been around since nearly the Wright Brothers if we didn't."

"Oh, really?" Dana was not at all convinced but enjoying the banter. "So you're saying small companies such as mine and large companies like yours have more in common than people think? Give me a concrete example, and *then* I'll tell you the name of that book."

Barry contemplated for only a split second.

"Well, getting it right is really important for us too." Barry had a look of satisfaction. "After all, I work for the company that built the plane we're sitting on."

"Then fasten your seat belt, mister." She grinned. "It could be a bumpy flight."

DISCUSSION QUESTIONS

CHAPTER ONE

1. If your team dedicated a song to you on the radio, what do you think it would be? Why?

2. One character suggests that Dana should be checking her e-mail over the weekend? Do you agree? If your company expects that, do they give employees the proper tools for working from home? Is such work expected to be done off-payroll?

3. Todd uses influence when telling Dana it's important for her to support the company's change initiatives. How important is the use of influence within your team or in your organization?

4. Dana says she thinks companies that lose sight of their core business often fail. Do you agree? Can you suggest ways in which companies can expand without losing their way? How important is it that management seeks buy-in from employees when adopting change strategies?

5. Dana seems concerned that Matt is being left out of discussions on the new direction of the company, even though she and Matt are not on the best of terms. Do you think people can balance tension in their personal lives with

what needs to be done to benefit the company as a whole? How?

CHAPTER TWO

1. Todd and Matt talk about the importance of building alliances between team members. Is that valued in your organization? Discuss some of the ways in which alliances can yield stronger results.

2. Dana complains that she doesn't get any respect either at work or at home. How important is being respected where you work? What are some things you could do to encourage more respect from your colleagues?

3. Nikki says she doesn't like when people aren't "authentic." What does being authentic mean to you? How can you inspire more authentic behavior in your own organization?

4. Matt talks about Dana's aversion to change. How important is it to embrace change in an organization? Can management in your company do things to communicate upcoming changes more effectively?

5. Nikki reminds Dana that new opportunities often accompany change initiatives. Discuss examples of how that has happened in your own experience. Is there more you can do to see those opportunities and benefit from them earlier?

CHAPTER THREE

1. Jeanne believes that managing organizational change is the biggest challenge facing companies today. Do you agree? Why or why not?

2. Dana says that many companies struggle with their need to maintain a balance between their history and their future. Have you found that to be the case in your own organization?

3. Nikki says that she thinks it's sad that many employees don't realize the impact they've had on a company until after they have left. Has that been your experience as well? What should companies do to regularly acknowledge employees' contributions?

4. The relationship between Matt and Dana is changing. Do you believe Matt's compliments are sincere, or do you suspect he has another agenda? Why?

5. The interaction between Dana and Todd becomes quite heated. Do you think either of them could have handled the situation better? How?

CHAPTER FOUR

1. Jeanne has said several times that her job is not managing the company but managing change. Does she have her priorities in order? Why or why not?

2. Jeanne Rasmussen tries to coax the company's newest employee into giving her a gauge of employee morale. Is there a better way to elicit this kind of information? Do you think Nikki was correct in being so frank with the CEO? Why or why not?

3. Do you think Dana's behavior with Matt and Todd is appropriate? Have you witnessed anything similar in your work experience? How could Dana have handled the situation better?

4. Nikki says her business wisdom comes from reading a lot of self-help books that have applications in the workplace. Are there books that you have bought to improve your personal life that you have used at work as well? What did you learn from them?

5. Do you think Dana has jumped to conclusions about the company needing to move to another location? Should she have been more careful with this information? What do you think the repercussions will be if her statement appears in the newspaper?

CHAPTER FIVE

1. Dana speaks several times about the importance of properly communicating a change initiative. Do you agree? Can you think of an example when your company communicated well? Poorly?

2. Nikki asks Dana what about changing the company is so threatening to her. Was that an appropriate question to ask her manager? Why or why not?

3. We deal with many clichés and adages in our everyday lives, from motivational posters at work to advertising campaigns. Can you think of some that you feel reflect your own values? How so?

4. Dana continues to voice concerns about her lack of trust among her team members. Are her fears justified? Can you think of ways in which her team leader could build trust in the workplace?

5. Nikki says that even though some people aren't the best communicators, their intentions may be good. What role do intentions play in your workplace? Can people's intentions be good while their actions are less so? How?

CHAPTER SIX

1. What do you think Nikki means about not allowing our thoughts to imprison us?

2. Dana seems to have a bias against what she calls "self-help" books. Have you ever found that genre of books to be useful in your workplace interactions?

3. Nikki says the key to any new behavior is how we use it during stressful situations. Do you agree? Can you think of examples when stress caused you to act poorly?

4. Do you think Peter acted in a trustworthy manner by telling Jeanne of his interaction with Dana? Should Dana have been upset about it?

5. Jeanne says everyone feels like a fraud from time to time. Do you think that's true? Can you give examples from your own life?

CHAPTER SEVEN

1. Nikki's roommate asks her if Dana was "blowing smoke" when she spoke about moving the company. Are there rumors you hear that make you wonder about the sources of the information? What role does office gossip play in your organization?

2. Nikki says that her roommate has been in the corporate world too long. Do you think people naturally become more cynical the longer they've been in an organization? Why or why not? What could management do to address the situation?

3. Do you agree with Nikki that people emulate the behavior of people they respect? Can you offer examples?

4. Dana's son told a lie to get something he wanted. Have you seen examples in your life of people lying to achieve their goals? How has that affected your behavior toward them?

5. What do you think Dana means when she says, "I have learned my lesson"?

CHAPTER EIGHT

1. Dana says social lies don't count. Do you agree? Have you used that rationale yourself? Did it make things easier, as Dana claims, or did it complicate things instead?

2. Nikki believes people need a history of success with new behavior before they commit to it long term. Do you agree? Why or why not?

3. Dana's son Chris appears more open to the idea of moving than anyone else. Do you think his age has something to do with it? Are older people less likely to accept change? Why or why not?

4. Dana calls Chris a "dreamer" but she doesn't mean that as a compliment. Are there dreamers in your company or in your life? How are they perceived?

5. What do you think will happen if the company decides to move to another location? What will that mean for its employees? Its customers? Are there, as Dana claims, certain areas of the country that are more hospitable to business than others? What happens to those areas that are not?

CHAPTER NINE

1. Dana apologizes to Matt for not carrying her own weight at the office due to family problems. Are there people in your company who are having trouble balancing their work and personal lives? Does the company do anything to help? Do you?

2.   Todd tells Peter that he predicts Dana will be late to the meeting. Was that professional? Why or why not?

3.   Dana says she feels it's sad that junior employees are often left out of important company decision making. Does that happen in your workplace? What can companies do to better include the viewpoints of new employees?

4.   Dana thanks Nikki for the gentle way she encouraged her to be more accepting of change. Should companies be more concerned with the way they communicate a need to change to their employees? How could they best do that?

5.   Do you agree with the four Lessons from the Hive that Nikki's mother sends? Why or why not?

A CONVERSATION
WITH THE AUTHOR

· ·

READERS ARE ALWAYS interested in learning more about
the creative process of authors—what inspired them to tell the
stories, what the messages were they were hoping to convey,
and how they hope their stories and experiences can help benefit the readers' understanding of the world around them or
tackle a particular challenge or conflict. Charles Decker took
a few minutes to answer some of these questions and wel-
comes your thoughts and comments to the story he told in
Lessons from the Hive. Who knows? Maybe one of your stories will inspire a future book?

*Charles, this is your second business fable based on a
real company. Why do you think this genre continues to be so
popular?*

As Dr. Beverly Kaye says in her Foreword, this type of
storytelling has been around since man has been able to communicate. People are always interested in stories, but it's only
recently that this genre has encompassed the workplace,
where most of us spend the greater part of our waking lives.
Managers are always looking for a nonthreatening way for
their staffs to relearn basic business skills, so this kind of
book fits the bill nicely.

If this story is based on a real company, as you say it is, why be coy? Why not just name the company?

You know, it's tempting, because these well-run companies deserve some good press. But after my first book, *Beans,* came out, I heard from many readers that not identifying the real coffee company better enabled them to imagine their own company as the one in the book. I've also heard from some readers that they enjoyed guessing the company that was the basis of the book. I got an e-mail last week from a reader in Taiwan who was going to Seattle to find it!

So are you prepared to reveal the name of the company you're talking about in Lessons from the Hive?

I will tell you, and no one else, that the stories my friends at Burt's Bees have told me over the years were the inspiration for the book itself. I love their products and their history. I use at least one of their products almost every day.

How closely does it parallel the story of Burt's Bees?

Most of the actual story is fiction, but Burt's Bees *did* have to move in order to grow, and they *did* add new product lines to their core business. Other than those similarities, the rest may or may not match their own experiences. I really can't say.

How long did it take to write the book, and how many of the characters are based on real people?

Writing the book took only about three months, but I had been thinking about the story for several years, including the time I was working on *Beans.* The characters came to me in a dream, actually, and fortunately they stayed with me afterwards. They are all based on real people, but some who read early versions of the book tell me it's more fun to imagine who would play the characters in a movie. I agree.

This mysterious self-help book with the yellow cover plays a major role in the main character's transformation. Are you going to tell us the name of the book or keep us guessing? Do you think these kinds of books can really make that much difference in changing people's attitudes?

It's funny. A friend who read an early draft of the manuscript remarked how clever it was of me to promote *this* book, with its yellow cover, in the text itself. But the one in the story is based on an actual book by an eminent doctor and therapist at Stanford University. If people really want to know, they have to e-mail me at cdecker@acumentum.info and I will tell them. And yes, I do believe in "bibliotherapy" as a way to keep one's problems at bay. As Nikki says, there's a lot of bad self-help out there, but there's some really good stuff too—and it has helped me personally quite a lot.

Nikki, the junior change agent in the book, obviously believes in the mantras that most people call clichés. Why do you think clichés are so often dismissed as pablum for the masses?

I don't know the answer to that, but it's worth considering. Most of us probably laugh at them because they remind us of our parents' admonitions when we were kids, but I think they certainly contain an element of truth. As Nikki observes, that's probably why they become clichés.

Dana talks about the importance of "getting things right." What do you think most companies are still not getting right?

In my opinion, after 25 years in corporate America, the one thing they still haven't gotten right is how to treat people. Employees are the lifeblood of any company, yet they are often treated as a bother rather than as a resource. It's sad. I only hope the fable books I write might make *one* manager behave better for just one day. Think about the millions of people who would go home happier, kiss their spouses, treat their children better, play with their pets longer. If these kinds of books can make a difference, then they have accomplished something very important indeed.

Can we look forward to another book from you?

Actually, I am working on two complementary books, as well as a sequel to *Beans.* So many people contacted my coauthor and me after we published *Beans* with their stories of how that book had impacted their lives, that we felt maybe a sequel would help many more. My own next book is about hiring good people, demanding better customer service, empowering employees, and encouraging customer loyalty. It's based on a real bakery chain called Au Bon Pain, which I personally think does a superb job on all those fronts. The working title is *The Staff of Life.* Get it?

ACKNOWLEDGMENTS

MANY PEOPLE HAVE been involved in the development of this story and this book. I couldn't begin to name them all, so let me issue a blanket thank you to those who offered advice and your own stories during the time this book was being written.

There are some who really stepped up during the last couple of years, a particularly difficult time for me. I am deeply indebted to Barbara Monteiro, Linda Chaput, Matthew Barnes, Sally Hertz, Bob Rosner, Bev Kaye, Leslie Yerkes, Brayton Bowen, John Williams, Chuck Lundeen, Jennie Coogan, and Neila Hingorani. My family has also been a tower of strength and understanding during this time. My appreciation is boundless.

I would like to extend a special debt of gratitude to the wonderful team at Dearborn Trade Publishing, including Roy Lipner, Paul Mallon, Cindy Zigmund, Leslie Banks, Courtney Goethals, Trey Thoelcke, and Eileen Johnson. I count them among my dearest friends. Jonathan Malysiak is any author's dream editor. I feel very lucky to have been introduced to him and his amazing editorial judgment.

Finally, I would like to thank the thousands of people living a variation of this story in countless organizations across the country and around the world. This is as much your story as it is mine.

ABOUT THE AUTHOR

CHARLES DECKER HAS been involved in virtually all aspects of business and professional publishing for more than 20 years. He is currently a consultant to the industry, as well as Vice President for Client Relations for Acumentum, Inc., a digital publisher based in New York City and San Francisco.

Recently he was a senior executive at Amazon.com in Seattle. He previously served as President and Publisher of Berrett-Koehler Communications in San Francisco, where he pioneered a series of shorter-format works designed specifically for the human resources, organizational development, and training markets.

He is a former Director of Doubleday's Executive Program book club, where he evaluated more than 2,000 business manuscripts each year for possible inclusion in the club. During that time, he received numerous accolades for his part in the launch of the Business Literacy program, which fosters group reading in corporations around the world.

He is the coauthor of the international bestseller *Beans: Four Principles for Running a Business in Good Times or Bad,* which has been translated into ten languages, and writes the monthly Readers' Choice column for *Fast Company* magazine. Profiled in the *Los Angeles Times* and *Across the Board* and

Inc. magazines, as well as the nationally broadcast *Business of Success* radio program, Charles lives in New York City.